STEAL, KILL & DESTROY

A Guide for Today's Christian on How to Disarm the Adversary

Written By:
Loribel Maldonado

Copyright © 2019 by Loribel Maldonado

All rights reserved. No part of this publication may be reproduced, distributed, or transmitted in any form or by any means, including photocopying, recording, or other electronic or mechanical methods, without the prior written permission of the publisher, except in the case of brief quotations embodied in critical reviews and certain other noncommercial uses permitted by copyright law. For permission requests, write to Loribel Maldonado via email at simplyloribel@icloud.com

Ordering Information:
Available wherever fine books are sold or online.
Available in E-Book format via select e-book platforms and providers
E-book ISBN: 978-0-9856835-8-0

Printed in the United States of America
ISBN 978-0-9856835-7-3
First Edition
14 13 12 11 10 / 10 9 8 7 6 5 4 3 2 1

All Scripture quotations are derived from the New King James Version (NKJV) of the bible unless otherwise noted.

Scriptures marked NKJV are taken from the NEW KING JAMES VERSION (NKJV): Scripture taken from the NEW KING JAMES VERSION®. Copyright© 1982 by Thomas Nelson, Inc. Used by permission. All rights reserved.

Cover Design by JRaah Media Group, LLC
"Design with Purpose to Glorify God." ©

This is a work of creative nonfiction. Some parts have been fictionalized in varying degrees, for various purposes. Any resemblance to actual persons, living or dead, or actual events is purely coincidental.

DEDICATION

I dedicate this book to Dr. Rochelle N. Oxendine who helped to ensure that I put the pen to the paper.
Thank you!

FOREWORD | THE ARMOR OF GOD

"10 Finally, be strong in the Lord and in his mighty power. 11 Put on the full armor of God, so that you can take your stand against the devil's schemes. 12 For our struggle is not against flesh and blood, but against the rulers, against the authorities, against the powers of this dark world and against the spiritual forces of evil in the heavenly realms."
Ephesians 6:10-12 New International Version (NIV)

  I have read this scripture countless times, and it is part of a passage that many people read when they go through hard times. We are in a fight for our lives, even when we cannot see it. The same battles that we read about in the Old Testament, the very ones waged in massive fields, are still happening today. The fight for deliverance and freedom from oppression from the hands of slave masters is still very real. Yes, we aren't walking over blood-soaked fields riddled with fallen soldiers in our daily lives; but we are trying to move forward, to walk past the fallen dreams, the letdowns, the guilt, and the failures. We fight to be free and away from the influence of slave masters who hurl condemnation, shame, and lies attached to the tip of their dividing tongues. We are in a fight where the conflict takes place in the mental and spiritual arena of our lives.

Throughout scripture, you see the effects and the wear of compromise on vision, as the enemy speaks partial truths via persuasive words that shift the destinies of the target audience. One conversation led by the words "*Did God really say*" nudged Adam and Eve to act on their desires to eat the very fruit God told them to stay away from. When they saw that it was good and pleasing to the eye, they took a step towards their sin. The Devil didn't force them to eat the fruit nor did he make them do it. They entertained the lie and walked right into the enemy's plan. After they sinned, God approached them, and the first thing that happened was that they began to play the blame game. Adam blamed God and Eve, and Eve blamed the devil. Yet, none of them took the time to search their own lives to ask "what part did *I* play in this?". Placing blame and pointing the finger at others or at the devil himself for the condition of our lives is taking the easy way out. To say, "the devil made me do it" to excuse a compromising moment isn't living truthfully. The truth may be a harder pill to swallow. As long as we keep blaming the devil for the fruit of our own actions, we will never break the cycle of sin and bondage over our lives. The enemy welcomes the blame because it enables the cycle of sin to continuously rule over us. Why is this so? It is because we won't take responsibility over our actions when we fail to ask ourselves, "what did *I* do in this situation?".

Ephesians 6:11 states, *"Finally, be strong in the Lord and in his mighty power. Put on the full armor of God, so that you can take your stand against the devil's schemes."* I read this wrong for many years of my life because I assumed schemes just meant lies; however, a scheme is a plan, a method, or an assignment. God has a plan for your life, and it is great, but remember, the enemy has a plan also, and it is to steal, kill, and destroy. It is with this understanding that I am so glad that Loribel Maldonado wrote this book "Steal Kill and Destroy: A Guide for Today's Christian on How to Disarm the Adversary." In these pages are truths that will help you fight back and win the fight. Steal Kill and Destroy is a flashlight that casts light into dark places, into mindsets, excuses, and fears. You will need two things while you read the following pages. First, you will need scuba gear because she takes the reader into deep waters. Second, you will need a hard hat as you enter your construction zone where excuses are demolished and hope rebuilt. This book isn't simply words on pages meant to decorate your bookshelf but an additional tool that you can use to fight the good fight of faith. I pray that as you read Loribel Maldonado's latest book that you will be encouraged, enlightened, empowered, and elated.

-Timothy McCain
Evangelist and Author

TABLE OF CONTENTS

INTRODUCTION i
CHAPTER 1 | KNOW YOUR ENEMY 1
CHAPTER 2 | WEAPONS OF MASS DISTRACTION & FOOL'S GOLD 25
CHAPTER 3 | WEAPONS OF MASS DISTRACTION CONTINUED 49
CHAPTER 4 | TRIED AND TRUE.. 67
CHAPTER 5 | B.C. MOMENTS 91
CHAPTER 6 | THE WEAPONS OF OUR WARFARE............ 105
CHAPTER 7 | IT IS FINISHED... 135
BIBLIOGRAPHY & WORKS CITED 149
ACKNOWLEDGEMENTS: 150
ABOUT THE AUTHOR 152
RECOMMENDED READINGS: 152

INTRODUCTION

There is a predator stalking the land. It walks across a plush, green field with its prey in tow. Every sway in its stride boasts of its long-awaited victory. The fawn's limp and lifeless body now lies in this fearless animal's mouth; it never stood a chance. The sac that nature intended for the protection of this defenseless creature is still visible. Still partially intact, it half-surrounds the fawn's fragile body. It cannot compete against the fierce, apex predator who lies in wait.

A stiff carcass now broadcasts the triumph of this predator to the pride. The blood of the lifeless creature crowns the victor. After having more than its fill, it turns to settle just a short distance away from the fawn's remains. Its appetite has been satiated, yet, its eyes carefully survey the plains for its next prey as its tongue savors the remaining crimson droplets from its lips.

All humans who live here on Earth are at the top of the food chain; no animal naturally hunts us as they hunt the fawn. However, we have a supernatural predator; if ignored, the consequences are lethal. I spent many of my adulthood years ignoring him. I eventually found myself contemplating how this world would not miss me very much if I were no longer around. That's when I first realized it: I was under attack. It was the bottom of the ninth and Satan was bringing in his version of the "closer" to the game.

Not today Satan.

I reflect on the many times I lost battles to the enemy because of my ignorance to his schemes. He almost had me there. I heard a man say once, "The devil is the devil not because of his power, but because he's been around longer". While this saying came not from the world's finest theologian, he has a point. I am convinced the devil wins more often because he has more knowledge than we do. *That* gives him an advantage. Ignorance is not bliss—it is dangerous. As the saying goes in the criminal justice system, "ignorance of the law is not a legal defense."

I will give you an example of what this means in layman's terms. Let's say someone from a different country visits the United States of America (USA). In his country, it is legal to exact vengeance on someone who has wronged you with no legal repercussions from the government in that country. While this man is visiting the USA, he feels wronged by a New Yorker who shoved him on a crowded mass transit platform.

This foreigner takes matters into his own hands and decides that the payment for this man's actions is to lose the very arm he used to shove him. He takes out a knife and chases after this man—and cuts his arm off. Shock and amazement seize him as the police place the handcuffs on his wrists. He stands before the judge at arraignment as he hears the charges against him.

He apologizes to the judge as he enters a plea of "not guilty". He rationalizes that he is a foreigner and is not aware of the rules, laws or customs governing the USA. He seeks a pardon, or maybe just a warning with no other ramifications. The judge looks at the man and pardons him by saying, "Oh okay, I completely understand. You are free to go. You didn't know. I dismiss this case."

No, that is not the way the legal system works in the USA because ignorance of the law is not a legal defense. Even though this man is just visiting, he is still subject to the rules and laws governing the land he is visiting; he is expected to abide by them. The judge will most likely shake his head in disapproval as he sets the date for the next court hearing and moves on to the next case on the docket.

Likewise, there are principles and biblical truths that, if not followed, allow the enemy to engage us at will. Just because you don't know the rules of engagement and ignorantly invite the thief into your home, it does not mean that he will not enter. Ignorance of what your position is in the Kingdom of God gives the enemy victory over the daily battles in this life.

The adversary has the advantage because of his knowledge, not because of his power. He has put in the time. He has spent generation after generation studying mankind. He's watched your ancestors repeatedly succumb to his time-tested tactics which have served him well. I'd like to assume many of our ancestors won some battles against the enemy. I would love to think because of those victories, it leaves the enemy with no other option but to come up with something new. Yet, I wonder if our ancestors ever passed down the knowledge gained from their victories. If they did, it never made it down to me. Instead of passing down old wives' tales and folklore, how to stand against the devil is what they should hand down.

The purpose of this book is not to make myself an expert on the devil's tactics because I am still learning to stand today. With this book, I take responsibility for the information I've received, and I pass that same information down to you, so pay attention. There is a desire burning inside of me to make sure that our future generations don't succumb to the tactics the enemy uses time and time again. A desire sparked after what seemed like endless anguish and suffering at the hands of a defeated foe. I got sick of losing, especially when I know the Word of God declares my victory in Christ. Yet in the first couple of years of my Christian walk, I wasn't feeling so victorious.

Aren't you tired of being sick and tired? Tired of the same old traps? It must end; it has to stop not only for you, but also your future generations. A good friend of mine shared some of his struggles with parenting in New York City (NYC). I discerned that he was fighting unnecessary battles. I realized all he had to do was shift his focus and take authority to speak change into that situation. To get him to understand his position in the kingdom, I asked him this:

"If a man walked up to you and your family and suddenly slaps one of your kids, would you let him?"

There was a pause on the line. I could only envision the snide look on his face as if saying, "What do you think would happen to him?"

I am leaving out his response, but we all know what it should be. No good parent would ever stand by and watch child abuse unfold right before their eyes, especially not by some random stranger with nothing better to do than to pick on a vulnerable child. I am sure the person would not walk away the same if he actually hurt them. With the raise of his hand, he would instantly become an enemy, period.

Please do not misinterpret what I am saying. This is not an invitation to incite violence amongst yourselves. Instead, I want to stimulate your thought process about this life and the world in which we stand. You would never stand by and watch as someone abuses another life – not yours, not that of your children, not the weak or the helpless. So why do you just stand there and let the devil do exactly that to you and your loved ones?

Take a stand against the devil. Take back everything that he stole over generations past. I pray that this book inspires you to reflect on your own life to examine areas where the enemy gained the upper hand. I pray that you receive a revelation of the enemy's tactics so you are equipped for future successes in those same areas. Fear not, for he is a defeated foe. God wants us to have victory here on Earth, not just in heaven. We are winning in the now because of what Jesus Christ did on the Cross. Jesus said, "It is finished," and it was not a reference to our lives. What is "finished" is the devil's dominion. We are victorious in Christ. It is time for us to take a stand and go after him who "steals, kills and destroys".

CHAPTER 1 | KNOW YOUR ENEMY

"If you know the enemy and know yourself, you need not fear the result of a hundred battles. If you know yourself but not the enemy, for every victory gained you will also suffer a defeat. If you know neither the enemy nor yourself, you will succumb in every battle."

(Sun Tzu).

here is an unholy trinity and together they are responsible for most of our daily struggles. Nathan Finochio, a teaching pastor at Hillsong NYC, writes on how this trio impedes the Christian's ability to hear God in his book *Hearing God* (Finochio, 2019). Likewise, Chip Ingram, Pastor and CEO of Living on the Edge, a discipleship ministry, touches on it in many of his teaching series. What I like about

CHAPTER 1 | KNOW YOUR ENEMY

Chip's teachings is that they are very practical and he communicates well on how to apply his teachings to your own life. However, when I speak of this trio, my aim is not to contradict their teaching, but to apply what I have learned so far. I will draw from their teachings, which I use as a supplement to God's word and never as a replacement. God's word is the primary source of information for this book.

The first party to this trinity is the **world** in which we live. Yes, you read that right, the world. You might say to me, "Loribel, what do you mean the world? God created the earth and everything in it. God also said it was *all good*! Did you skip that part in the great book?"

My response to your keen observations is this, yes, the world *was* good but not anymore. Now it is a byproduct of the enemy's reign over it. I will go over the enemy's tactics and what the world's role is in his plan for you later on in this book. First, I want to shed some background on what I am talking about and what we are up against. For some of you, this may seem elementary, but I gear this book towards a wide audience so let us be patient as I lay the groundwork.

God gave Adam dominion over the earth and everything in it. Adam signed over his rights to this world when he chose sin over righteousness. Jesus took back dominion when He laid His life down on the Cross and rose from the dead on the third day. However, prior to His victorious ascension into the heavens before He took up the Cross, and just before He started His ministry, Jesus also faced temptation by the devil. The manner in which the devil tempted Jesus is the same way he tempted Eve, and it is also how he tempts us today.

Google™ defines temptation as "the desire to do something, especially something wrong or unwise" (Temptation). Therefore, in order for something to be a temptation to you, you must first have a desire for it. Otherwise, it's not a temptation. Therefore, in his efforts to get Jesus off His divine assignment, Satan took Him up to a very high place. He showed Jesus all the kingdoms of the world and offered them to Him. Who was Jesus here to save? The world—that is why it was a true temptation. Matthew describes it in Matthew 4:8-9 (NKJV):

> *8 Again the devil took Him up on an exceedingly high mountain, and showed Him all the kingdoms of the world and their glory.*
>
> *9 And he said to Him, "All these things I will give You if You will fall down and worship me."*

CHAPTER 1 | KNOW YOUR ENEMY

The devil cannot offer what he does not have and the world, at the time, was his. Jesus came to save the world and so when Satan offered Jesus the world, it was a true temptation. But there is a catch! There is always a catch. I am referring to the whole worshipping Satan part—yes, that catch. That would be the "unwise" aspect of the temptation previously defined. The devil half-offered what Jesus would eventually get on His own through obedience to the Father. Satan offers shortcuts and all the glory without the process for the low, low price of rebellion. All Jesus has to do in exchange is rebel against the Father, ignore God's word, and worship Satan.

However, Jesus cannot ignore that which He already is! He is the Word made flesh. It was only when Jesus spoke a rhema word to the devil that the devil is disarmed. After, the testing there is always a time for refreshing. Jesus is refreshed and ready for His ministry. Jesus, concludes his earthly assignment by overcoming the world and all of its troubles. John 16:33 (NKJV) confirms it. If the world were not an adversary, then what would there be to overcome?

Next in this unholy trinity is the **flesh**. Yes, the flesh that houses your soul and spirit is an enemy. The Word reads in Romans 8:7 (NKJV) that *"the carnal mind is **enmity** against God; for it is not subject to the law of God, nor indeed can be."* The flesh is self-pleasing, self-fulfilling, and is after its own desires. It is not interested in the things of God.

Do you think it's the enemy that suddenly makes you sleepy when you open up the Bible? There is no mistake—that is the flesh and not the enemy. He is not that powerful. Do you know the level of effort it would take for the devil who is not omnipotent (all powerful), not omniscient (all knowing), and definitely not omnipresent (to be everywhere at once), to attack you every time you open the Bible? No matter how supernatural he may be, he does not have that ability.

Trust me when I tell you, it is not him. It's your flesh—that same flesh that will let you binge on Netflix™ for hours past midnight on a work night —*and* somehow you miraculously make it to work on time the next day —will cause you to feel more tired at 7pm when you open up your Word to read it. Why is that? Because the flesh naturally opposes the things of God. That is why Paul, in the book of Galatians, lets us know what walking in the flesh looks like versus walking in the Spirit: so, we can discern for ourselves in which spirit we are walking in. Let's look at Galatians chapter 5 verses 16-21 (NKJV).

16 I say then: Walk in the Spirit, and you shall not fulfill the lust of the flesh.

CHAPTER 1 | KNOW YOUR ENEMY

17 For the flesh lusts against the Spirit, and the Spirit against the flesh; and these are contrary to one another, so that you do not do the things that you wish.

18 But if you are led by the Spirit, you are not under the law."

19 Now the works of the flesh are evident, which are: adultery, fornication, uncleanness, lewdness,

20 idolatry, sorcery, hatred, contentions, jealousies, outbursts of wrath, selfish ambitions, dissensions, heresies,

21 envy, murders, drunkenness, revelries, and the like; of which I tell you beforehand, just as I also told you in time past, that those who practice such things will not inherit the kingdom of God."

Wait, so you are telling me that the devil did not cause me step out of my marriage (adultery)? The devil did not drive me to have sex before marriage (fornication)? The devil did not force me to cuss out that driver who cut me off on the expressway (outbursts of wrath)? No—he did not. It was your flesh.

I have had many outbursts of wrath—in those moments, I was not walking in the Spirit of

God at all. I was in the flesh. Especially if I felt as if I was being treated unfairly or when I witnessed some injustice. That is when my skin would boil. Outbursts of this type are not of the Spirit. It is not the same as the righteous anger that Jesus speaks about. There is no edification in this anger nor does it provoke positive outcomes for anyone. If left untreated, it can bring with it sorrow and destruction. I recall that during my final months as a child protective investigator (CPI), I experienced more and more of these outbursts. The last outburst left me so deflated.

    I remember it like it was yesterday. The grace for me to continue in the role of a CPI was seemingly lifted and I found everything about the job irritating, especially when I did not feel supported. I felt that we, the advocates of the most vulnerable population in the community we served, needed advocates of our own. It also seemed to me that the sense of urgency for the work we did was not visible in the works of others across the board. I began to experience feelings of anger, disappointment, and resentment, which made me short and irritable all the time. Most of all, I felt drained with almost zero energy to focus on the things that were more important. All of this because I shifted my focus off God and His design for me and onto imperfect beings no better than I was. To top it off, I put a high expectation on them, which only led to more disappointment. It was a vicious cycle.

CHAPTER 1 | KNOW YOUR ENEMY

Emotions that were rooted in resentment began to spring up inside of me. Looking back on this now, I see that my feelings about the work I did changed after a series of unpleasant events. I wanted to go into "full-time ministry" yet, it was not in God's timing. I began to feel that maybe moving my family to Florida was a mistake. I started listening to the voice of doubt in my mind that said maybe God did not choose me. The more I focused on that voice, the louder it became. I followed the voice to the supposed "realization": "I *am* rejected by the Almighty." This undoubtedly dealt a hearty wound to my heart. Out of that wound emerged the seed of resentment that anchored its roots deeper into my being. It's crazy because the Lord warned me this was happening through a dream (He has always spoken to me through dreams) and I made little sense of it until now.

I dreamt I was sitting on my bed, which at the time faced the door. From my side of the bed, I could see down the hallway that led into the living room. A small, black Chihuahua-like dog jumped on my bed and I began to pet it, as it was friendly. This Chihuahua turned its attention to something outside of my bedroom door. I immediately glanced up to see what had this dog's attention and saw a shadow hurry down the hall. I jumped off the bed and hurried after it. As I headed down the hall, I saw the garage door was ajar so I went to it. As I opened the door, I saw a tall man dressed in a deputy's uniform hovering over the front end of my work-issued vehicle.

I saw that he was from the Sheriff's Office, so I asked him what was he doing in my house and under what authority. He remained defiantly silent, so I asked him for his name so I could report him. His demeanor unchanged, still refusing to say a word, I yanked on his uniform shirt from the area right above his right pocket where his name tag was and pulled him into the living room. I yanked his name tag off him and released him just for a moment while I looked at his name. It read "Resentment, A." I looked up from his tag and into his stone-cold face. I grew angry inside and yelled as loud as I could, *"you don't belong here; get out!"*

I turned to open the front door so I could push him out of my house. The moment my back was turned to him, he pulled me from behind and dragged me back to my room. Before we made it back, I woke up on my bed with my heart still racing. That morning, I googled the definition of resentment. Google™ defines it as "bitter indignation at having been treated unfairly" (Resentment). Over the next few months, those feelings would manifest and grow stronger in me with every passing day at the workplace.

I started to feel at work as if the harder I worked, the more it went unnoticed. I tried to

CHAPTER 1 | KNOW YOUR ENEMY

advance in the workplace, but my efforts were futile. To avoid the impending separation from my job, I even tried to transfer out of the division, but the doors seemed to be welded shut. I was making appropriate safety determinations for the children on my caseload only to have my efforts thwarted, which eventually placed the child back at risk. I felt as if I was fighting a losing battle. I was feeling the pressure that the Israelites experienced in captivity when they were made to produce bricks without the straw.

Soon, the fruit of this seed became evident in my daily speech about the workplace. Words that used to be pleasant to hear had become bitter. I went from being the comforter to my coworkers to the one in need of comfort. Out of the abundance of the heart, the mouth speaks (Matthew 12:34 NKJV). I was indignant; with my words, I started to feed a self-promoting ego that steadily grew stronger inside of me. Once the ego steps in, God steps out — it's that simple. Just like that, I opened the door to the enemy, who then seized the opportunity to advance in my workplace. He turned up the heat, my caseload nearly doubled and suddenly, the job I once found so much pleasure in felt more and more like hell. Sound familiar?

I learned in anger management over a decade ago (yes, I took that class and if you relate to what I am saying, maybe you should too) that I cannot control the actions of others and can only control my reaction to them. That is what I seemed to have forgotten—nonetheless the Holy Spirit convicted me shortly after my last outburst. I had a Christian co-worker who I started to turn to instead of God for advice. Holy Spirit showed me after my last rant that she wasn't necessarily living true to Proverbs 17:9 and neither was I. God is gracious and forgiving. He forgives me and so I forgive, simple as that. Complaining and murmuring, or, in my case, explosive moments of wrath, will only leave you wandering in the wilderness with no way out.

I realized that ranting to my co-worker friend fixed nothing. That day, I went home and turned my direction to God. I identified that at the core, I was uncharacteristically operating in the flesh. I had been doing it for some time and it was clear. As I write this, it's been such a long time since I last experienced an uncontrolled, emotional response to anything. This was a classic "Before Christ (B.C.) Moment," yet I am in the "Anno Domini (A.D.)" present. (For more on my "B.C. Moments," see Chapter 5.) What really made things clear for me in that period was reading the book of Galatians.

The number one way to know when you are walking in the flesh is with the measure found in the book of Galatians. After reading it, if you relate to my experiences, I encourage you to ask God for

CHAPTER 1 | KNOW YOUR ENEMY

the right spirit. In Galatians 5:22-26 (NKJV) Paul describes in verse 22 what the opposite of walking in the flesh is, which is walking in the Spirit. He says that the latter looks more like this:

> 22 *"But the fruit of the Spirit is love, joy, peace, long-suffering, kindness, goodness, faithfulness,*
>
> 23 *gentleness, self-control."* (There it is self-control—if you lack control, you, my friend, are in the flesh.) *"Against such there is no law.*
>
> 24 *And those who are Christ's have crucified the flesh with its passions and desires.*
>
> 25 *If we live in the Spirit, let us also walk in the Spirit.*
>
> 26 *Let us not become conceited, provoking one another, envying one another."*

Amen!

Last in the unholy trinity is the **devil** himself and all of his minions (and by "minions", I mean "demons"). Let's turn to the book of Ezekiel for a closer look at the former attributes of our adversary. The chapter is lengthy, but I encourage you to read Ezekiel 28:11-19 (NKJV) in its entirety for yourself. Don't just take my word for it. There, you find a description of Satan as **"the seal of perfection"** who in his glory days had every precious stone as his covering as he walked back and forth amid fiery stones.

He was "perfect" until God found iniquity in him. Verse 17 reads that "his heart was lifted up because of his beauty" and that he "corrupted his wisdom for the sake of his splendor." Satan's *pride* was the cause of his fall, and it's what often comes before destruction, as King Solomon states in Proverbs 16:18.

Whenever you hear someone say prideful or boastful statements, watch out! Destruction is on the way. What was Satan's sin? Pride. There are many levels of sin, but I think pride ranks right up there with murder. Pride is destructive and is at the root of many sins. Pride is at the bottom of most failed relationships. There is a very popular movement today named after this very sin. It is called "gay pride" which is like a cocktail of many sins in one. Gay pride embodies the sin of rebellion, sexual perversion, vanity, and pride itself just to name a few. Unfortunately, all sin regardless of classification, lead to destruction.

So how do you deal with a sinner? You share the truth of the Gospel. You share the truth in love. Perfect love casts out all fear and love keeps no record of wrong. You are to share the

CHAPTER 1 | KNOW YOUR ENEMY

truth of the Gospel and what it means to be loved and accepted by Jesus Christ. Acceptance is not tolerance. Tolerance means that you allow something despite your opposition to it. Jesus does not tolerate us He loves us. He desires a deeper connection, so he offers us salvation at the cost of repentance; through repentance He accepts us into Him. While acceptance means that He receives us just as we are, the love of Christ is a transforming love that loves too deeply to leave us in the same sinful state that He found us in. Through His love and sacrifice, He transfers us from the kingdom of darkness and into the Kingdom of Heaven. This means that when we accept Jesus, we receive a new identity. The more we fellowship with God, the clearer this identity becomes. It is then that we go from the corruptible to the incorruptible.

Satan was corrupted by his pride. Isaiah 14:12-14 (NKJV) gives us a glimpse of just how boastful the devil became because of his corrupted state of mind:

> *12 How you are fallen from heaven, O Lucifer, son of the morning! How you are cutdown to the ground, you who weakened the nations!*
>
> *13 For you have said in your heart: 'I will ascend into heaven, I will exalt my throne above the stars of God; I will also sit on*

the mount of the congregation On the farthest sides of the north;

14 I will ascend above the heights of the clouds, I will be like the Most High."

The devil—a created thing—wants to be the Creator. He wants to play God. For that, God cast him out of Heaven, and now, Satan is on the path to his demise. Before he arrives at his final destination—a fiery lake — he wants you to come along.

It is important for you to realize that the devil hates *all* of humanity including those who willingly commit to his way of life. He hates you and I because we have something he does not. Because of his pride, he's Heaven's outcast. His relationship with the Almighty has forever been severed. He did the unpardonable, and in so doing, he brought a third of the angels down with him. He will never regain his glory.

His job was to minister unto the Father in the heavens. He was Heaven's worship leader. Now, he's fired and humanity has taken over his job. Ever since we replaced him, he is relentless in his pursuit to sever the relationship between God and man at all costs. His first attempt was in the Garden of Eden. He succeeded in his first strike, but his blow was not one that God did not already

CHAPTER 1 | KNOW YOUR ENEMY

expect. God has a plan for a Savior, and his name is Jesus.

I cannot stress enough that Satan is not all-powerful, nor is he all-knowing. Trust and believe that he was very much shocked at the unveiling of the plan of redemption through the blood of Jesus Christ. The birth of a Messiah was foretold, and it is how he perceived a savior was on the way, but he did not understand the specific details of God's plan of redemption. Still, he took a defensive stand with his limited understanding and set in motion a plan to kill the Savior of the world.

It begins as we read Matthew Chapter 2:1-7 (NKJV).

> *1 Now after Jesus was born in Bethlehem of Judea in the days of Herod the king, behold, wise men from the East came to Jerusalem,*
>
> *2 saying, "Where is He who has been born King of the Jews? For we have seen His star in the East and have come to worship Him."*
>
> *3 When Herod the king heard this, he was troubled, and all Jerusalem with him.*
>
> *4 And when he had gathered all the chief priests and scribes of the people together,*

he inquired of them where the Christ was to be born.

5 So, they said to him, "In Bethlehem of Judea, for thus it is written by the prophet:

6 'BUT YOU, BETHLEHEM, IN THE LAND OF JUDAH, ARE NOT THE LEAST AMONG THE RULERS OF JUDAH; FOR OUT OF YOU SHALL COME A RULER WHO WILL SHEPHERD MY PEOPLE ISRAEL.'"

7 "Then Herod, when he had secretly called the wise men, determined from them what time the star appeared."

Herod is instrumental to the enemy's defensive strike. However, what I would like for you to take notice of here in this text is that it also illustrates the devil's inability to know all things in the way that God is all-knowing. Satan knows some things but *not* everything. The Bible evidences this because Satan did not know the exact time and place of Jesus' birth or His whereabouts. If he did, he would have passed this information on to Herod. He gained that information by manipulation and deception. He incites Herod by planting a seed of fear in him. Herod fears losing a kingdom that was never his to begin with. He did not want a predestined king to take over his position. Therefore, to protect his

CHAPTER 1 | KNOW YOUR ENEMY

position as king, he gathers the priests and wise men for an inquiry. His goal is to learn two things: the "where" and the "when": *where* is the savior and *when* did he arrive?

Once Herod gathered the information needed, he sent the wise men out to gather the proof of life. He further instructed them to return to him with confirmation of their encounter. Verses 8-9 continue:

> 8 *"And he sent them to Bethlehem and said, "Go and search carefully for the young Child, and when you have found Him, bring back word to me, that I may come and worship Him also."*
>
> 9 *When they heard the king, they departed..."*

Although the enemy has a plan in motion to destroy Jesus' destiny, God, who is all-knowing, remains ahead. If by chance you stopped reading right here, you would probably worry about what would happen next. Will the wise men reveal Jesus' location? Will baby Jesus be safe? I can almost see King Herod back at his palace thinking to himself, "Yes, I've got him now. Once the Magi return, I will know where the Child is and then I will kill him." Herod thought his victory was certain. *But God...*

God is not about to let the enemy gain the upper hand. Romans 8:29 says that those He foreknew He also predestined, meaning He has already mapped it all out and has already prepared a counterattack to all of the enemy's tactics. God always has a plan. First Corinthians 10:13 (NKJV) states that God will always make a way of escape.

After the wise men encountered Jesus, they received a divine warning via a dream not to go back to King Herod as originally planned. By obeying God's warning, they disarmed the devil. Sometimes, all you need to disarm the devil is a little obedience, and obedience is at times simply to listen to the warnings God so faithfully provides. It will disarm the devil, and that weapon will not prosper!

Isaiah 54:17 (NKJV) says that no weapon formed against us will prosper, but I wonder how many of us read the previous verse. Verse 16 points to God as the Creator of all things, including the one who is forming that weapon (the blacksmith) against you. This does not mean that God is purposely forging weapons against you. What this verse does is it reminds us that God is sovereign and God has control over all things even those things that afflict you. He is not surprised when things happen, in fact he already has a plan to help you overcome. I love it how God always has a way of pointing back to his sovereignty. It's like

CHAPTER 1 | KNOW YOUR ENEMY

He's saying never forget the God that you serve. He is all powerful, all knowing, and omnipresent. God says in Jeremiah 32:27 (NKJV):

> *"Behold, I am the LORD, the God of all flesh. Is there anything too hard for Me?"*

I love the assurance that I receive from that text. It is invigorating to know that nothing, and I mean nothing, will have victory over me because I serve the most-high God.

It was not enough for the Lord to divert the wise men; He also warned Joseph. The story goes on to say that Joseph left Bethlehem and moved to Egypt until Herod was no longer a threat to Jesus. I encourage you to read the remaining chapter for yourself. Not only does Chapter 2 show us how the enemy operates, but it shows us his weaknesses. I want you to realize that the enemy operates on old information. Since the intel is old, he cannot succeed, because God is always making things new. It is not surprising to me that another one of his weapons is to always bring up the past. This is because he cannot entirely see the future.

Once King Herod realized the wise men would not return to him and armed with only the location and approximate age of the foretold King of the Jews, he made a decree. He ordered that all children in Bethlehem under the age of two be put to death to assure his reign over the Jews. A lot of planning went into this scheme. It was cold, cunning, and elaborate, yet it wasn't new.

The adage that says "You can't teach an old dog new tricks" probably speaks of the devil. He had used this tactic before during the time of Moses' birth. Instead of King Herod, the leader of that time was the Pharaoh of Egypt. You'd think he would learn from his failures, yet this plan, like the plan to kill Moses, also failed. It's back to the drawing board for you, Satan. The enemy is never victorious—at least not for long. Know that we have everlasting victory in Christ Jesus. Amen.

Like Jesus, we have a great purpose and design that we must carry out. Jesus said that we will do far greater things than He did. If the enemy tried to kill Moses and Jesus before either of them could walk, what do you suppose his plan of attack is for you today? Modern day Satan does not need a pharaoh or a king to do his bidding. He continues to go back to the drawing board to redesign his weapon with new and improved technological advances.

The process is now streamlined, so all Satan needs is a few misguided souls to believe his lies. His weapon of choice against children is abortions. Please do not misunderstand what I am saying, the term abortion is a very broad term. I am discussing abortion as a weapon of the enemy. What I am not discussing is the person who has

CHAPTER 1 | KNOW YOUR ENEMY

made a decision to have an abortion. I am not on the judgment seat here. I am talking about the deliberate act of abortions for personal gain at the expense of an innocent life. I wonder how many future ministers, pastors, evangelists, apostles, teachers, and prophets are not with us today because of it. For the ones who survived the pre-birth attack, Satan has a Plan B[1], pun intended. (More on his weapons of choice in Chapters 2 and 3.)

And what about those who have fallen into the schemes of the devil and have had abortions in the past? Well, the Bible says Jesus came to redeem the Fall of Man. With His redemption came forgiveness. Jesus dealt with the problem of sin once and for all. The Word says in Colossians 2:14 (NKJV) that Jesus:

> *"...disarmed principalities and powers, He made a public spectacle of them, triumphing over them in it."*

To understand the greatness of God, it is important to take Him out of the limitations of our concept of time. God stands outside of time and is

---

[1] "Plan B is a progestin-only emergency contraception product that helps prevent pregnancy when taken within 72 hours of unprotected sex" (FAQs: Plan B One-Step®.)

not limited by it, either. When Jesus disarmed the principalities and its powers, I believe the weapon of abortion was included. Therefore, although I do not yet see it, I am convinced the victory is God's, and in Jesus' name, He has redeemed those affected by abortion. Our victory is in Christ. Not only are we victorious, but we daily face an unarmed, and defeated foe. His artillery, like his time, is limited. Satan has very little left in his arsenal to win the battles against you and me; he knows the war is over.

At the redemption of mankind, the enemy's plan for humanity disintegrated, and boy, is he mad! Not only did we take his job, but now our sins are forever forgiven and we are redeemed. Not his. We are pardoned, forgiven, and made joint heirs with Jesus Christ, and he is not. He will never join the saints in Heaven. Every time he sees us, it reminds him of this. He is on death row. All he can do is try to take as many people down with him as possible.

When I worked in the Corrections field, I asked why a man on death row was referred to as a dead man walking" by other inmates. A senior corrections officer told me; they are dead men walking because their fate is sealed with the penalty for their crime. Because of this, they are facing a death sentence in prison.

CHAPTER 1 | KNOW YOUR ENEMY

 We regard these to be the most dangerous inmates to supervise, because they have nothing to lose. They have nothing but time to sit and plot. Depending on how they feel, they may plot ways to take as many people down with them as possible. Because of the penalty they face, their hearts may become hardened and their demeanor is both fearless and merciless. They may develop deep-seated hatred for others and can become ruthless and have no remorse for their actions. That is how your enemy, the devil is, as well. He is a dead man walking and he's after *you*!

CHAPTER 2 | WEAPONS OF MASS DISTRACTION & FOOL'S GOLD

"Be sober, be vigilant; because your adversary the devil walks about like a roaring lion, seeking whom he may devour."
1 Peter 5:8 NKJV

he trick that the enemy has always used in my life since I was a kid has been fool's gold. This is when you get off course for the sake of "something better", thereby the call on your life is postponed. Fool's gold is nothing but a distraction of the devil. It is frustrating. While I know God's will manifests despite the enemy's schemes, I can't help but think God's will would have manifested sooner had I not fallen for Satan's fool's gold; but that is just my impatience talking.

I tread lightly here because God is all-knowing, and it does not surprise Him when these

CHAPTER 2 | WEAPONS OF MASS DISTRACTION & FOOLS GOLD

things happen to us. Fully knowing this, I still don't like the enemy to gain any territory or any small victories when he is already a defeated foe. He does not deserve any freebies from me. If he is taking anything, let's make it hard. While God is totally in control here, we still have our part to do to ensure that His will comes to fruition. God commands us to be sober and vigilant. So, just because God is all-knowing and all-powerful, and He has a plan in place already to redeem our losses, it does not negate the fact that He commands us to take action and to take a stand against the wiles of the enemy. Let us not forget that inaction is still an action.

Jesus commands us to be vigilant. That means we have to watch, observe, and analyze what is before us. We must learn to distinguish the real from the fake. It requires discernment, as sometimes you must distinguish the right from the almost-right. Sometimes, it takes experience. Have you ever been "hoodwinked", tricked, or deceived? Trickery is the devil's specialty. I must admit that I have fallen victim to this scheme more times than I can count. An example is when I was about 14 or 15 years old. I was walking on Lexington Avenue towards the 125th Street 4,5,6 train station as an unsavory character approached me. He did this in the same way you see it on television, minus the creepy hat and the long trench coat. Instead of walking away from him, I entertained him.

STEAL, KILL & DESTROY

Out of one of his pockets, he took out a shiny Italian gold Figaro chain with an anchor and rope pendant. The style was popular and I was in the "I want to be cool" phase of my life. He said to me that he was facing financial hardship, yada-yada-yada, and before I knew it, I handed him $40 cash for the chain. You must think $40 is nothing—well at the time, I was working for minimum wage and earned only $4.25 per hour. I never worked more than maybe 25 hours weekly, so I handed him about half of my earnings for that week. What's worse is that my mother relied on these earnings to supplement the needs of the home. Forty dollars went a long way back then. Afterwards, he handed me the chain and promptly bolted in the other direction.

That was all in a New York Minute, folks! I blinked, and he was gone. I was left there wondering why he left so fast. I reasoned that he must have been on his way to feed those hungry kids. Too excited to care about where he went, I could not wait to get back to the block and show off my brand-new chain. My happiness was short-lived when I got back to the block and met with my friends. As I showed off my necklace they immediately called it a fake. I pretended to know it was a fake as I did not want to lose the "street cred" by admitting I got "got".

Later, I visited the corner pawn shop and showed the necklace to the clerk who, with one glance at it, confirmed it was a fake. I tossed the chain and then lied to my mother about what I had done with my money that week. I was absent-minded during that period, so to tell my mother I lost money was not very far-fetched. I was not about to admit that a stranger tricked me. I mean, who would do that to a 14-year-old girl? There is a reason for the warning, "Never talk to strangers", yet I entertained the stranger's voice. I believed his lies, and the experience resulted in a loss.

Have you ever listened to the voice of a stranger over the voice of God? Jesus says in John 10:27 that *"My sheep hear my voice, and I know them, and they follow me."* Maybe if my relationship with God was a closer one or if I was more in tune with His leading, I would have heard the warning. God doesn't want to see you take a loss, no matter how insignificant it may be to others. God cares about all of the things that matter to you.

Now, I will not over-spiritualize that experience, but it could have easily opened the door to doubt and mistrust in me. It is subtle things like that which give way to the enemy to inch his way into total dominion over your life. If after that experience I became more distrusting of people, jaded, or if my heart was hardened to the needs of others, then it would have been a victory for the enemy. This is because the next time someone would've come to me with a need, I would not have responded the way the Lord desires. He wants us to be representatives of His hands and feet. Thankfully, I did not let this situation harden my heart to the needs of others. Besides, it is likely that the man depended on some controlled substance which dictated his actions and clouded his reasoning. I will not blame him, because he is also a victim in this example. I use this to illustrate how Satan likes to distract you from your life's calling and desires by dangling a fake, shiny replacement blessing before you to distract you from the real thing.

There are desires we are born with, and I know they are divine. Satan's job is to take those desires, twist them, pervert them, or completely distract you from them. Ever since I was a child, there lived inside of me a desire to teach, yet those desires did not come into fruition until I was 39 years old. My desires deferred because of a simple act of treachery—a bait-and-switch act of the devil, if you will. I ignored the gift of teaching that was within me because I was trying to impress or be better than others. Don't be fooled; if the enemy discerns your gifting while you are still young, he will stop at nothing to ensure you do not get off to a right start.

I grew up in a home with four other sisters. It is easy to become invisible in a household with many children competing for the love and affection of a single mother. We grew up in poverty and although we didn't really know it, (as only adults

CHAPTER 2 | WEAPONS OF MASS DISTRACTION & FOOLS GOLD

notice those things) it became very clear to me that we were poor as we got older. I just thought we lived the same way that most people lived. When I finished fifth grade, my mother sent my sister and I to visit my grandmother's Spanish Harlem apartment for the summer. My mother fell on some hard times shortly after this visit. After some discussions between the adults, we returned home only to pack our bags. Off we went to my grandmother's house for good.

The move to Grandma's didn't mean we hit the jackpot; we were still poor. The move just meant they divided the load. I honestly didn't know we were poor, although we went to the check cashing store every beginning and middle of the month to collect a government check and paper food stamps. While we did not live in luxury at Grandma's, she was spiritually rich, and we were happy, believe it or not, despite all of her rules. It was at my grandmother's house that I learned about God. She was Pentecostal, and so that made me a Pentecostal too. I formed a relationship with God via a third party.

Relationships formed with God in this way can sometimes leave a lasting impression and a healthy fear of God in you, but they never last. At the first opportunity to fall back into your old ways, you will. This relationship via a third party is superficial and is not suitable for long-term sustainability, because there is no root. I encourage you to take this time to reflect on the basis of your relationship with God.

Are you serving Him because it is the cool thing to do? (Believe it or not, there are people today who think it's cool to dress like a hipster pastor and wear cool merch with inspirational spiritual quotes.) Or are you serving God to gain the affection of the opposite sex? If you fall into any of these categories, meaning, your motivation to serve God is something other than the realization that you are at a loss without Him, then I suggest you stop reading this right here. Do not pass go; do not collect $200!

This book will be useless to you unless you repent from whatever other force is driving you to serve God and refocus on Him alone. Without devotion, there's only deception. Ask God to reveal to you through His Holy Spirit what it means to have a solid relationship with Him. Only then are you going to stand against the enemy's tactics. Amen?

Then, let's move on.

It wasn't until my sister and I started middle school that the realization of our economic status slapped me right in the face. One day, after school, as my sister and I walked home, we heard some kids chanting "Two-for-a-dollar shoes", as they pointed and laughed at our shoes. Yes, we got our shoes from the dollar store. I remember when we picked them out. We were so excited and proud of our new, shiny, patent leather loafers. All of my affection for the shoes quickly faded with the chant of every syllable escaping their lips. "Two-for-a-dollar shoes!"

My heart beat in my throat at the realization. We hurried home, yet it took me a whole 24 hours to process. The next day, I was so emotional that I cried in the schoolyard. I did not share my feelings with my grandmother. Why would I make her feel bad for something she could not control? We were poor, simple as that, or so we thought! Poverty is a generational curse. Jesus releases us from these curses, thanks to the power in His blood. He made Himself a curse for us when He took up the Cross. That is what Jeremiah was talking about in Chapter 31:29-30. It was a foreshadow of the freedom and redemption we receive through salvation in Jesus Christ. I will not go into much detail on blessings and curses, but as a reference, you should check out Deuteronomy 28. Also check out the materials written by a well-known Christian authority on this subject, Derek Prince. Although Derek Prince has passed on to be with the Lord, there are YouTube videos of him teaching on this very subject. I strongly urge you to read it if you are experiencing the effects of a generational curse over your life.

This childhood experience unknowingly impacted my life as an adult. I never wanted to lack a single thing. It also made me very materialistic by nature. There is nothing wrong with having material things. There is a problem when those material things become little "g" gods. My love and affection for material gain is something God has always worked on with me. After I surrendered my life to Christ, I left a six-figure income job for a lesser paying one to "prove" I was no longer attached to material gains or economic status. The truth about my attachment to material things slapped me in the face when I decided to donate clothes and items I no longer used since my move to Florida.

I remember as I looked at each item, I would try to justify a reason I would "need" it in the future, and tried to save it. I had a pair of three-hundred-dollar, water-resistant, winter UGG© boots that I debated on whether to keep or not. My husband would shout at me, "We live in *Florida!*" to remind me we were not going to face any snowstorms in the near future. In the end, I got rid of over six bags of clothes as well as dozens of shoes and accessories I no longer had use for, but I was still holding onto. I literally cried as I went through each item. I realized the reason I held onto material things is that I never again wanted to be in want or be made fun of for not having the latest of the trendiest brands.

Jesus said in Matthew 19:24 that it is easier for a camel to pass through the eye of a needle than it is for a rich person to enter to the Kingdom of God. Do not misinterpret this passage. God is

CHAPTER 2 | WEAPONS OF MASS DISTRACTION & FOOLS GOLD

not opposed to material wealth; He is opposed if it stands between you and Him. In the preceding verses, a young man who seemingly obeyed the law and did the "right" things asked Jesus what "good" things he must do to obtain eternal life. Jesus instructed the young man to keep the commandments and the young man said he did. Jesus then responded to him to sell his belongings, give them to the poor, and then follow Him. The young man was saddened by this, because he had great wealth.

Jesus, by asking him to do this, was proving a point. The young man said that he kept all of God's command when it was not so. Jesus is not opposed to wealth, but Jesus sees what's at the core of all things. This man's wealth had become a little "g" god before him, which directly violated the 1st of the 10 Commandments given to Moses: *"You shall have no other gods before me"* (Exodus 20:2 NIV). This young man valued his wealth over God; that is why he was sad. Therefore, his wealth was exalted to the position of a god to him. God wants to prosper us, but not at the expense of your salvation. Many are asking God for wealth and enlarged territories but do not receive it because He sees what the effects of such an increase would be on your life.

As Christians, we need to embody the attitude of Shadrach, Meshach, and Abednego. They were so confident in the Lord that they were satisfied knowing that God decides their fate. God was still God if he saved them and *"even if he doesn't"* save them, God's decision will not dethrone Him in their lives. God's response to their trouble did not determine His identity as God. He should be the only deity sitting on the thrones of our lives. Yet, how many of us are quick to blame God when we don't get our way? God will enrich and enlarge territories as He sees fit to do. What my purge experience showed me is that even though I walked away from a six-figure income job, deep down inside, I was still very much attached to material things.

Now, I live my life as humbly as I can. I still struggle with the temptation to store up material things. Even as we speak right now, I have to do another purging session to get rid of unnecessary things around my home that I have unwittingly kept this past year. Moving forward, I will say as Agur the son of Jake in Proverbs 30:7-9:

> *7 Two things I request of You (Deprive me not before I die):*
>
> *8 Remove falsehood and lies far from me; Give me neither poverty nor riches—Feed me with the food allotted to me;*
>
> *9 Lest I be full and deny You, And say, "Who is the LORD?" Or lest I be poor and steal, And profane the name of my God."*

CHAPTER 2 | WEAPONS OF MASS DISTRACTION & FOOLS GOLD

At my grandmother's, there weren't many things to keep me entertained. We didn't have cable and Wi-Fi was not yet a thing. Our television options consisted of channels 2 through 13 and the two Spanish language channels of 41 and 47. Still, we managed with what we had because we did not know any other way. I could not play outside because all that surrounded our apartment building were burnt buildings that the homeless or drug users occupied. So, to keep myself busy, I would write poems, sing, or be of service to my grandmother or my grandmother's neighbors, whom we knew from church. Most of all, my favorite pastime was to pretend I was a teacher. I would line up teddy bears and pretend they were my students. I would also pretend with my sister, and we would take turns being the teacher.

Sometimes my mother would visit us at Grandma's. On these visits, we would share our grades and our achievements, trying to make her proud. Pride is another destiny-blocker. I sought my mother's favor at all costs and wanted to be better than my sisters. Naturally, when my sister shared with my mother that she wanted to be a teacher when she grew up, I wanted to one-up her and said I wanted to be a doctor. That was short-lived as it later changed to wanting to become a lawyer because of my natural ability to argue points. Afterward, I went back to wanting to be a doctor and finally ended with the choice to be a heart surgeon. No one could top that.

Despite my stated desire to be in the medical field, my favorite game to play with my sisters or stuffed animals was the teacher game. I don't think I ever played the role of a doctor or a lawyer. I would line up my stuffed animals and teach them what I learned in school. I loved school so much that I would wake up on Saturdays, astounded that there was no school. Yes, I was that kid that reminded the teachers they had not given a homework assignment the night before a holiday or a weekend. Some kids in school would make fun of me and would call me names like "Brainiac", but I did not care. One teacher shared with me a phrase that I would chant back whenever the kids would start back up again. "Sticks and stones may break my bones, but words will never hurt me." It worked for me because their words never hurt me.

The desire to learn and to teach others what I learned has always been in my DNA. For now, I will fast forward past the struggle of the teenage years and young adulthood to where I reunited with God. I shared this snippet of my childhood to point out that despite my young desires to teach; I didn't. I never even vocalized it. Life happened. I got distracted. I let the circumstances of life dictate the direction of my future. Most of all, I began to doubt that I could become anything

CHAPTER 2 | WEAPONS OF MASS DISTRACTION & FOOLS GOLD

remotely indicative of success. Doubt is another weapon of mass distraction.

James, in Chapter 1, verse 6 of his book in the New Testament, tells us that the one who doubts is like a wave of the sea, blown and tossed by the wind. That is exactly what my life was like. I was so filled with doubt, worthlessness, and lack of identity that I took a passive approach to life. I began to simply exist. Passivity is another weapon that distracts us from God's intended plan. I wasn't rolling with the punches; I was letting life happen as if I did not have another option. I tossed here and there, taking a pounding from left to right. I started to exist without hope for a future.

My life and God's plans for it took form when I reconciled with the Lord. But this did not happen until I was well into my 30s. I pray that this serves as an encouragement to all who are praying for the lost and for family members who have turned away from the faith. The Lord hears your prayers, and He is faithful to fulfill them. God is not a man that he should lie nor a son of man that he should change his mind. His word does not return void—meaning it goes from Him and does not return until it fulfills its intended purpose. It has been my experience that although for a time I turned away and rejected the Lord, He still held up His end of the deal and never wrote me off as lost. Instead, He was patient and met me exactly where I was, and He showed up exactly when I needed him.

Another thing that happened when I finally rededicated myself to the Lord is that the Holy Spirit filled me with an insatiable desire to learn the Word for myself. I started to take online Bible college classes that helped lay the foundation for me. The classes were free and while I did not receive credits towards a degree; the teachings were solid. It was on this slow yet steady walk with Christ that the Lord began to transform my heart. He conformed my sights to perfect alignment with His will for my life. The enemy thought he deterred me from God's intended purpose for me, but God will not be shaken. He is not done with me and He is definitely not done with you! If you are reading this and you feel that you have missed it, you didn't. Let God move in His perfect timing. All you have to do is be still, be patient, and move only when you see Him move.

The closer I got to God, the more I wanted to share my experiences with others. This book is a prime example of that—I am sharing what I have learned so far in this walk. Yet, before I could shout from the rooftops what God has done for me, I needed to find a church home. After searching for what seemed like an eternity for the right church home, my cousin-in-law introduced me to Hillsong NYC. My home away from home. There, I felt welcomed and it was exactly the environment I needed to grow in God's word. The

CHAPTER 2 | WEAPONS OF MASS DISTRACTION & FOOLS GOLD

Lord orders our steps and, as if on cue, Hillsong NYC began offering evening college classes with Pastor Nathan Finochio.

It was during my studies there that I read the Bible for the first time from cover to cover. True to the teaching nature within me, I would take what I learned and in turn would share it with my family at home during our independent Bible study times. I would ask Pastor Nathan for resources and he would make suggestions of books I should read. From his suggestions, I would find others. One book and one resource at a time, a foundation was forming. That is how my faith began to grow.

Eventually, the Lord course-corrected my path. I am back to writing for His Glory and not my own. And wouldn't you know it, as of this writing, I recently started a teaching career! It took over 20 years, but, praise the Lord; I am back on the right path. I am still taking continual Bible classes. God willing, by this same time next year, I will have a bachelor's degree in theology. I've learned in this walk that the more I get to know the Word, the closer I get to God. It is through the knowledge of the Word that I can spot the enemy's tactics over my life more effectively. The more I read the Word, the more my faith is strengthened. In it, I am forever reminded of who my God is and how limited the devil is. As we take a deeper look at the enemy's tactics, remember that God is the only limitless one. Satan has limits in what he can do to you.

We see this in the life of Job. In order for you to get some context of what I am about to say, please read Job Chapter 1. Here, Satan stood before God, who asked him if he had considered Job. God did not ask this so that Job would be under the fire. No, there was a process Job needed to go through. Many theologians have varying views on the life of Job and what really brought on this testing. Some say he endured the trials he did because Job knew his children were in sin and did not address it. The belief further denotes that God values all life and the fact that Job would offer sacrifices to atone for the sins of his children, even the ones he wasn't sure they committed, was in itself a sinful act, especially since it is believed he never brought correction to his children for it.

While I don't disagree with this school of thought, I lean more towards the school of thought which notes that deep down inside of him, Job saw himself as more righteous than most. I think he had a prescriptive approach to his faith. What I mean by this is that he followed all the rules and knew what to do just in case he fell into sin to get back into God's grace. Job is of the Old Testament and was under the old covenant. If one sinned, the law demanded the sinner present a sin offering before the Lord in accordance to the law, so that it would be forgiven.

CHAPTER 2 | WEAPONS OF MASS DISTRACTION & FOOLS GOLD

The problem with the old covenant is that this process never dealt with the root cause for sin. For many, it became just another religious ritual. I also believe Job was comfortable and relied on his own righteousness so much so that it may have automated his relationship with God. That is just my view of it, and I am not dogmatic about it because I am flawed. Since it is not clearly stated in the Bible, one can only speculate. Job was very comfortable in his righteousness. Underneath the surface of the image others knew of him, there may have been some feelings of self-reliance and pride. A correction would require a shift in the condition of his heart that only God could bring.

In the beginning of his trials when asked about his afflictions, Job responds with the textbook replies one would expect from a man of his stature. They sounded like the responses of many Christians who today say only what they think is the right thing to say in the face of adversity, while never exposing the heart of the matter. Their homes are falling apart, their kids have rebelled, their finances are a mess, and when you ask them how they are doing, their response is, "I am just blessed and highly favored!" Really? That doesn't look like favor to me. It looks like there is an obvious need, yet I wouldn't know it, your Pastor wouldn't know it, and no one can stand in the gap for you because the devil has you telling everyone that you are "too blessed to be stressed." This in itself is a tactic of the devil to keep you alone behind the facade that everything is as it should be and away from those who will stand with you in prayer to expose and confront this attack.

There's nothing wrong with calling a horse a horse; if you are in pain, say so. This way, it can be dealt with. The number one way to defeat the enemy is to expose him. It will never be considered ungodly to admit it. There is a difference between identifying the affliction so it can be dealt with and letting that affliction steal your peace and joy. You can still remain in complete peace with assurance that God will see you through any affliction despite having said you are afflicted. See Philippians 4:6 & Philippians 4:19.

It wasn't until Job could no longer withstand his affliction that his true feelings surfaced. He began to rebuke the Lord's actions by seeing them unjust in his own eyes. Solomon asked in Proverbs 20:9 (NIV) *"Who can say, I have kept my heart pure; I am clean without sin?"* Solomon poses the rhetorical questions because no one can say that. Yet, Job began to see this season as punishment without cause. Job wanted God to answer to *him and provide him* an account as to why He was punishing him. Job considered himself to be a righteous man of God who followed the law and therefore saw no cause for grief and strife. It was in this moment that God stepped in and brought correction. He is very clear in both

CHAPTER 2 | WEAPONS OF MASS DISTRACTION & FOOLS GOLD

the old and the New Testament. We *all fall short* of the glory of God; we have *all sinned*, and this includes Job. The Lord said in Isaiah 64:6 that man's righteousness is as filthy rags before God.

God reminded Job of His omnipotence because, evidently, Job forgot. I would not want God to lecture me the way he lectured Job. I think I would die. But it is important to know that God brings correction to those He loves. Despite it all, God loves Job. Correction doesn't make you feel warm and fuzzy inside, but it will push you to the next level. In the end, Job is restored. Everything he lost in the process was given back to him with interest. The story of Job is very difficult to wrap your mind around, but I think that the process was necessary in order to elevate him to the position God desired for him.

I was recently on the receiving end of God's correction. After the grace lifted in my previous role as a CPI, I diligently looked for work. I renewed my credentials as a fraud examiner and commenced to sharpen my Anti-Money Laundering (AML) Skills, as that is my background. After many unanswered applications, I felt that maybe I missed it —I was out of the field for too long to jump back in. When I finally got a call back from a small bank near the Orlando area, I was walking on air. The pay was comparable, and the commute from home wasn't bad. I aced the phone interview, and I was on my way to a second interview.

Everyone knows that if you make it to the second interview, you are golden. I am superb at interviews and I thought for sure I had this in the bag. I went to work with a pep in my step thinking I had for sure gotten the job. About a week later, I received the "Dear John" phone call from this company, except we weren't even in relationship. The company went with another applicant. This has never happened to me before. My hopes of leaving such an intense line of work vanished just like that. I have always been very dramatic, but I must admit, my response to this rejection was far from a godly one.

I literally threw myself on the bathroom floor, phone still in hand having just received the bad news. I let out a gut-wrenching cry. "Why God? Why are **You doing** this to me? I thought you *were* a **good** God! Why would you leave me in a place when **you know I cannot take it anymore**?!" I sounded just like Job. I had the audacity to ask God "why?". As the words materialized in this realm, I felt the sting. I went too far. It was like the time I called my mother the improper pronoun for "you" in Spanish. I addressed her as "tú" instead of the formal "usted." My grandmother immediately slapped me across the face to serve as a reminder that my mother and I were not equal. Except, my grandmother was not here to correct me on this. I immediately went numb. I stopped crying and dusted myself off before getting dressed for work. I

CHAPTER 2 | WEAPONS OF MASS DISTRACTION & FOOLS GOLD

got into my work-issued car and off I went. I can't say for sure what I did that day, but I know this; on the silent ride home, the Lord spoke to me through a memory.

It was a memory from 2 years prior on the day I got a call from Human Resources (HR) informing me that they chose me to fill the position I was now dying to leave. I saw myself in my car on the phone with Shelly. As soon as I hung up the phone, I shouted, "Hallelujah!" from the top of my lungs. I was so happy, I immediately turned up the worship music and began to praise God for the answered prayer. When the memory reel finished, the rebuke came in a voice similar to mine that said:

"What happened to *that* hallelujah?"

God brought correction.

I immediately started to cry, and I asked God to forgive me. As I prayed, I took on the attitude of gratitude. I began to thank God for his mercy and grace, but most of all, I thanked Him for His faithfulness despite my lack thereof. I also asked Him to grace me with the ability to stay at this job and for the grace to do His will; I would do whatever His desire for me was, even if it meant staying there. These moments of correction are not fun because it is like when you get scolded by your parents, only worse. When God does it, you are instantly reminded of your mortality and of His sovereignty and quickly learn how insignificant you are in contrast. God is sovereign. He doesn't need us—it is the other way around. Know that if the Lord scolds you, it is because He loves you. His word says so in Hebrews 12:6-11.

I imagine the enemy must have publicized my dramatic meltdown in 4K[2]. It was not my finest hour. I realized I had brought on that battle to myself because like Job, I began to rely on my abilities. I left the spirit realm long ago and was operating in the flesh, meaning I was working in my own strength. I also became prideful and relied on my competencies, my work experience, my skills and knowledge rather than on God. This was also during a period where I worked very long days and got swamped with cases so much so that I began to work on my days off just to catch up. I was praying less and less, and I was *not* reading the Word.

Like Job, my repentance brought restoration. There was a true shift in the condition of my heart. There was a humbling that took place in me. This was followed by the realization that God is God because He *is*. He is all powerful and nothing exists that can match Him. In His mercy

---

[2] 4K "(in digital television and cinematography) technology, equipment, or content providing a very sharp image quality, with a horizontal screen resolution of around 4000 pixels." (4K)

for me, He still opened a door leading me out of the line of work that was wearing me out, even though I was undeserving of it. He went as far as to provide financial provision so I could walk away from my role as a CPI and finally step into His rest. He is **Good** and not because I said it but because **He is**.

CHAPTER 3 | WEAPONS OF MASS DISTRACTION CONTINUED

The enemy said, I will pursue, I will overtake, I will divide the spoil; my lust shall be satisfied upon them; I will draw my sword, my hand shall destroy them.
(Exodus 15:9)

When it came time for me to write on the weapons of mass distraction, the enemy unwittingly gave me material. Before going to bed on the night before I was scheduled to write this chapter, there was an inner voice that questioned the reason for writing this book. I could almost hear that voice ask me, "Who do *you* think you are?"

The next morning, I woke up, and I grabbed my cellphone. Usually, my vice is emails, but since

CHAPTER 3 | WEAPONS OF MASS DISTRACTION CONTINUED

I hadn't worked in weeks, I went straight to social media! I found myself on my Instagram page. I scrolled aimlessly and before I realized it, I scrolled myself right into Before Christ (B.C.) pictures. I never take them down because I don't pretend to have lived a "holier-than-thou" life before giving my heart to God. I saw pictures of friends I don't see anymore, people whom I cared deeply for and once upon a time, we were inseparable, but now, we are not. I suffered pangs in my stomach as I continued to scroll and before I knew it, there it was staring right back at me. It was a picture from 2006, the year that I missed it as a parent. I cried. The torment of the past. While the enemy uses many weapons, I think in this season this is the one that hurts.

Why does our adversary do this? His purpose is to enslave us. The past is a prison designed to keep us bound to things, moments, ideas, arguments, people, actions or inactions that we no longer have power over. He uses the past as a weapon to breed unforgiveness so that we ourselves in turn are not forgiven. Here is what God did for me: He healed me of the wounds from the past. He has rewritten my future. I can forgive because I am forgiven. Jesus has healed my wounds from the past and those very wounds are transformed into the testimony that I use today to defeat the enemy. Do not despise your past, as it is part of who you are today. It is your testimony. Revelations 12:11 says that the devil is defeated by the power of the blood of the Lamb *and* the power of your testimony! The devil tries to use the weapon of the past against you when really, it's your very own weapon to wield against him, so take it back!

What does your adversary want? He wants *you*! In Luke 22:31 Jesus said to Peter:

> *"... Indeed, Satan has asked for you, that he may sift you as wheat." (NKJV)*

This passage illustrates that Satan is relentless in his pursuit. Surely, at the time of this passage, Peter is walking with the Lord. You would think Satan would give up and move on to someone else—but, no. The closer you get to God you become a bigger threat to the enemy. Satan has a one-track mind and he is fixated on severing our union with God. He wants to destroy what he cannot have. He also wants to prove God made a mistake in choosing you over Satan. However, Satan cannot just do anything to you; he needs permission. That is why Jesus says, "Satan has asked for you." Satan discerned a character flaw in Peter, and he was chomping at the bit to get at him. The only time that the enemy does not need permission is when you have made *provisions* for him yourself. God sets the limits on what the devil can do because your Creator knows what you can bear. If the devil comes in like a flood, then the Lord will raise up a standard against him (Isaiah 59:19).

The enemy welcomes opportunities to make you stray from your intended path, whereas the Lord sees those very opportunities as a time for the strengthening and conditioning of your faith. It is God's bootcamp, but only those who are being prepared for war go to bootcamp. Count it all joy when you go through these trials and tribulations, because it is the testing of your faith that forms perseverance. Paul says in the book of Romans, Chapter 5 that:

"tribulation produces perseverance; and perseverance, character; and character, hope."

One thing I admire in soldiers after they have survived boot camp is their stature. They are six feet taller when they come back from bootcamp. They are more confident, thanks to all the training they received. Tribulations are like bootcamp training for us and in bootcamp, not everyone makes it through. Some go and quit as soon as it gets too tough to bear. The same thing happens to new Christians. They dedicate their lives to God and because of the misconceptions usually associated with conversion, they fall back to their old way of life at the first sign of trouble, which usually takes place the same day of conversion or shortly thereafter. I remember the day I rededicated my life to the Lord. My husband and I got into one of the biggest fights we've ever had that it caused me to wonder whether we would make it out of Las Vegas alive.

I call this a shaking. The moment of your conversion, you are immediately transferred from the kingdom of darkness into the kingdom of Heaven. In the process, your old dwelling place is demolished and construction for the new home is underway. Before we build any structure, there must be a foundation in place to support the new structure. This foundation is created and reinforced with the Word of God. Many skip this step, and that is why they lose many battles quickly because they lack a solid foundation. The only word they draw from is the one heard during a Sunday message. I always heard Pastor Carl Lentz say on Sundays that the Bible works just as

CHAPTER 3 | WEAPONS OF MASS DISTRACTION CONTINUED

well on a Monday as it does on a Sunday. My advice to you is, don't rely solely on the teachings of others; you have got to read the Word for yourself.

I pray that after reading this book, you will have an insatiable desire to know the Word of God so that when you enter these training seasons, you will see them through to victory, armed with the Word as your guide. Faith comes by hearing and hearing by the Word of God (Romans 10:17). Therefore, let the Word of God be a lamp unto your feet (Psalm 119:105) as you navigate toward your victory.

There are plenty of Scripture verses quoted here and I encourage you to pick up your Bible and read them for yourself. I pray they equip you with the assurance that God is mightier than anything that will ever rise against you. No matter what weapon the enemy may forge against you, remember the words of Isaiah 54:16-17 (NKJV).

The devil wants nothing more than to prove that you are unworthy of God's love and affection. He feels wronged and because of his pride he does not see the error of his ways; or worse, he sees it and does not care. Most of all, he seeks to prove a point and he wants to use you as exhibit A.

STEAL, KILL & DESTROY

He wants to prove that those created to be lesser than angels are worthless creatures. It appalls him that such lowly creatures have authority over him and his kingdom. He thinks he is worthy of praise. He wants to control you so badly and fool you into thinking he is more powerful than what he actually is. He desires to take your worship and redirect it onto anything other than God. Worship was his thing and you and I are not counted as worthy enough in his eyes to carry out such a prestigious act. He prefers it if he were the object of your affection and will pull all the stops to get it; most of all he wants to be your god. There are many things he uses to usurp God.

How will he do it? He lies in wait, he tempts, he deceives, he causes even the elect to fall. Should the elect succumb to his schemes, he will then boast of his triumph over them by openly publicizing their failure. He desires to ridicule humanity in the presence of God and humiliate them the way he's forever been humiliated because of his pride. Satan is a great publicist. However, it is not your achievements he promotes, but your shortcomings instead.

CHAPTER 3 | WEAPONS OF MASS DISTRACTION CONTINUED

His name is **"the accuser"** in the book of Revelation for a reason. He daily accuses us before our Father, hoping that God will change his mind about us. He hopes that God will take His forgiveness away and that He would cast us into the lake of fire along with Satan. He is sad and doesn't want to go down alone. Don't feel sorry for him. It is *you* he is talking about. It is *your family*, *your destiny*, and *your freedom* he is after.

When Satan accuses us in the heavenly courts, God turns to our defense attorney, Jesus, and no longer sees us or our shortcomings. He only sees the righteousness of Jesus, and not our sins. There was a transfer of sin from us to Him. He took on our sins as we received His righteousness. He paid our debt in full. The penalty for sin is death, and Jesus has already picked up the tab. He did so with His own life on the Cross. By accepting the gift of salvation, you died to yourself and are now alive in Christ. We find salvation in Him. Your life is hidden in Christ's life; Colossians 3:3 says so. I believe it and so should you. That is the gift of grace. This means that when Satan is busy accusing you, God the Father, only sees the righteousness of Jesus Christ in you.

Don't get it twisted though, the devil is a force to reckon with because he is merciless and can bring with him a fury that humanity has never known. However, he is still no match for our God. The book of Isaiah mentions an unknown group of persons who will gaze upon the devil and wonder about him. I like to think you and I will be among them. Isaiah Chapter 14:15-19 tells it like this:

> *15 Yet you [Satan] shall be brought down to Sheol, to the lowest depths of the Pit.*
>
> *16 Those who see you will gaze at you, And consider you, saying: 'Is this the man*
>
> *17 who made the earth tremble, Who shook kingdoms, Who made the world as a wilderness And destroyed its cities, Who did not open the house of his prisoners?"*
>
> *18 All the kings of the nations, all of them, sleep in glory, Everyone in his own house;*
>
> *19 But you are cast out of your grave Like an abominable branch, Like the garment of those who are slain, Thrust*

through with a sword, who go down to the stones of the pit, Like a corpse trodden underfoot." (NKJV)

I love it! I can only imagine how the saints in the heavens gathered around just before God expelled Satan into the lake of fire. I get excited when I think of how we will marvel in disbelief and say as we point to Satan, "Is this the guy?" The devil is far bigger in our minds than in actuality; especially when compared to the greatness of our God. He has many tricks in his bag, so if you don't recognize any of the ones I will mention, take an inventory of your life, and ask the Holy Spirit to point out to you what the devil's weapons against you are in this season.

Awareness of the enemy's schemes helps us to disarm him. The enemy doesn't care if you are a child who loves God or an adult. He doesn't see your age, He sees your potential, your destiny, and automatically classifies you as a threat and goes after you. He strikes even when you are in your youth. I was not even old enough to walk when the enemy set his eyes on me. I sometimes get discouraged when I reflect on this. To make matters worse, my ignorance to his schemes delayed so many victories and blessings. I don't know about you, but I don't like it and it has happened one time too many times for my liking (hence, this book).

Ever heard of the saying, "If it isn't broke, don't fix it"? That is how Satan operates. He uses the same old tricks on unsuspecting victims. Like the unsavory character in my previous story, he sells us fool's gold. He may even go as far as dressing it up in a shiny gold-plated something as he tries to pass it off as real. He is the world's first counterfeiter. He takes the things of God and perverts them into his own version of them to confuse people. I will not lie; I have had a lifetime of getting tricked like this by the devil and the older I got, the more it cost me. The most expensive loss suffered is time. I've lost precious time. It is the only commodity we can never get back. If he can take your time, it is the cherry on top.

He fills up our schedules and our time with weapons of mass distraction. His tricks do not change, and while he does not use the same tactics on everyone, the goal is still to steal, kill and destroy that very thing God deposited in you before He formed you in your mother's womb. Let's go over his modus operandi or MO for short. It is his preferred way of operating—his most notorious

CHAPTER 3 | WEAPONS OF MASS DISTRACTION CONTINUED

attributes. This list is not all-inclusive, but I will note the major ones here. Please note these are not in any specific order.

He is a murderer, a liar, and an accuser (John 8:44). In the book of Revelation, Chapter 12, verse 10, Satan is named as the accuser. He tempts, he mocks, he deceives, he confuses with half-truths, he destroys, he steals, he bribes. He is untrustworthy because he betrays. Jesus implied in John 6:70 that one disciple was a devil (He was referring to Judah because of his betrayal). The enemy perverts (Acts 13:10); he sets traps and ensnares (1 Timothy 3:7 & 2 Timothy 2:26); he imprisons (Rev 2:10); he causes people to become prideful (1 Timothy 3:6); and he binds (Luke 13:16).

It is important to remember that while Satan has an arsenal of weapons, God limits him. I call his ammunition *weapons of mass distraction* because they keep you from your intended purpose if they succeed. That is why Jesus stressed to the disciples the importance of remaining vigilant. He described the enemy as a roaring lion, seeking whom he may devour. He's busy and never tires because it is worth it to him to stop you. He knows that God's plans for you are big and he can't risk the chance of you fulfilling God's destined purpose for your life.

He never knows the details of God's plans, but he gets intel from observations and from the things we say and do. We ourselves do not know the plans God has for us either. But God does, and in Jeremiah 29:11, He declares it. If we knew the plans God has for us in their entirety, there would be no room for faith. The Word of God reveals that without faith it is impossible to please Him (Hebrews 11:6). Therefore, it is incorrect to think we know the plans. I do, however, believe we have the blueprint within us with Holy Spirit serving as our guide towards God's design. Holy Spirit knows! First Corinthians 2:11 confirms it.

The blueprint is also the reason some feel empty inside, although they may gain money, fame, and success. If they have not lived out God's intended purpose for their lives, the emptiness remains and usually they live void of long-lasting peace and happiness. It is only through a relationship with God Almighty that we can achieve fulfillment. Therefore, despite all their gains, they still lead unfulfilled lives. This plus loss, abuse, rejection and emptiness are at the root of addictions. Most of the people we classify as the rich and famous suffer from these

CHAPTER 3 | WEAPONS OF MASS DISTRACTION CONTINUED

symptoms and dive face-first into a world that offers to fill this void via the use of recreational drugs and alcohol amongst other things. If left untreated, these will lead to the destruction of lives, marriages, families, and bright futures.

My first dive into this world was right after middle school, I moved back in with my mother. It was liberating because my grandmother had so many rules mixed with religion that it got to where if you sneezed, you were going to hell. Ok, I am exaggerating a bit for emphasis, but that is how it felt. Leaving my grandmother's house marked me because when I stepped foot out of her home that night, I left behind religion, as well. I wanted nothing to do with it. That is about as long as my relationship with God via a third party lasted. Over 20 years would pass before I ever considered full conversion into Christianity. Still, that seed my grandmother sowed would reap its harvest in due time. In those days, I strayed from the Word and drowned the desires that were once so fired up inside of me for God with the cares of the world. This was yet another weapon of mass distraction.

I recall that we lived in a Tier II housing facility for what seemed like an eternity. We ended up staying there for a little over a year. I started to hang out with the wrong crowd, and I went from being someone who was socially awkward to someone who was more accepted. Even after having left my grandmother's house, my mother always encouraged us to keep in contact with her despite my reservations about her. If all decisions led straight to hell while living with my grandmother, what would she think of me now? Therefore, I avoided those conversations like the plague.

Then one day, I had a talk with my grandmother; it was one of the last conversations I had with her before she died. The exchange was pleasant. She even shared a recipe for *sofrito* with me. We laughed and shared; it was beautiful. Before the conversation concluded, I had to ask why this conversation was different. She said she heard the Lord say to her He would save us, and she believed it. Because she believed it, she stopped badgering us. She did not get to see me come back to God in her lifetime, as I came back to God almost a decade after her passing, but I know she will know when she sees us in Heaven.

My Grandmother is a prime example of how damaging legalism and fear can be to the Christian faith. Legalism is a weapon of the enemy, as it makes this walk much harder than it needs to be. We see a prime example of how the enemy has been using legalism as a weapon against us in the ministry of Jesus Christ. In John 8:44, Jesus is speaking to the Pharisees, who were legalistic, and He said they were of the devil. You might wonder how He could say this to them when all the Pharisees did was study the Law of Moses, and they lived to ensure it was followed. The Pharisees knew the letter of the Law but they were far from the Spirit of the Law. Knowing the Law, just like knowing the Word of God, doesn't mean you are saved. Even Satan knows the Word. The devil knows the Word better than you and I. Jesus said to them:

"You are of your father the devil, and the desires of your father you want to do. He was a murderer from the beginning, and does not stand in the truth, because there is no truth in him. When he speaks a lie, he speaks from his own resources, for he is a liar and the father of it." (John 8:44 NKJV)

In this instance, Jesus said the Pharisees were after fulfilling the desires of Satan because they wanted to ensnare Jesus so it would justify their pursuit to discredit Him as the Messiah. If they could get Jesus to say or do something that was against the Law of Moses, then they would be justified in raising formal accusations against Him. Legalism prevented them from seeing the awaited Messiah in the flesh. The fear of what the truth could mean to their livelihood and their "way" of life was bigger than their desire for the Messiah in the first place. It was a successful weapon of the enemy back then, and it is still very prevalent today.

Today, legalism is the cause of Christians backsliding or turning away from the faith, because it is too hard. Legalism, like the shiny chain, looks good on the surface. It almost looks like the real thing, but it is not. Jesus did not like legalism, all throughout the New Testament He confronts it to bring correction to the legalist's theology. It is my belief that legalistic folk have not fully surrendered the "self" to God upon conversion and operate under the premise that their actions result in their righteousness, and not the fact that we are the righteousness of God via transfer from Jesus onto us. I pray the scales are removed from the eyes of every person operating under a legalistic spirit in the same way Paul's scales were removed from his eyes once Ananias prayed for him, in Jesus name. (Acts 9:17-18)

Legalism takes the focus off of God and onto actions and works. One of the hardest things to do

CHAPTER 3 | WEAPONS OF MASS DISTRACTION CONTINUED

is to yield our control over to the Lord. To fully step into the rest of God knowing that it is the complete work of the Cross that saves and not the other way around, is the only way to win against legalistic views. The only viable solution to legalism is complete and total surrender to God.

CHAPTER 4 | TRIED AND TRUE

For all that is in the world—the lust of the flesh, the lust of the eyes, and the pride of life—is not of the Father...
(1 John 2:16)

I can't imagine that the Devil has sufficient power and resources to go after every single person in this world. As much as he desires to be God, he isn't, and therefore he lacks the attributes that make God who He is. The devil is not all-knowing (omniscient), all-powerful (omnipotent) or everywhere at once (omnipresent). While the devil is seemingly limited in his schemes, he has a vast army to help him carry out his offensive strikes. This army is effective because they have mastered the art of carrying out their marching orders and they see them through to success. They are united

CHAPTER 4 | TRIED AND TRUE

and not easily divided unlike the body of Christ. It is important for the body of Christ to stand united as one against the devil the same way the devil's army stands united against us. It helps that the devil's schemes are always the same, as the devil does not have any new tricks. He may dress them up to change the outward appearance. However, the root of his attacks will always stem from these three things: *the lust of the flesh, the lust of the eyes*, and *the pride of life.*

The first time the enemy put this plan in motion was in the book of Genesis, Chapter 3. The first ingredient in most of his attacks is doubt in the form of a question. Chapter three begins with a description of the adversary: *"Now the serpent was more cunning than any beast of the field which the LORD God had made."* The key word here is *cunning*. Your adversary, the devil, is a cunning creature. Google™ defines cunning as "having or showing the skill in achieving one's ends by deceit or evasion" (Cunning).

I presume that Eve was caught off guard by a talking serpent because she seems confused in her response to him. Let this encounter between Eve and the serpent serve as an example of the enemy's timing in his attack. He will always strike when you least expect it. Jesus knew this tactic of the devil and tried to warn us in 1st Peter 5:8 *"Be sober, be vigilant; because your adversary the devil walks about like a roaring lion, seeking whom he may devour."* The disciples were in constant fellowship with the Lord Jesus Christ, yet they were still subject to the warning. Adam and Eve dwelled in the Garden's safety, where they maintained constant fellowship with the Lord. What could go wrong? Yet, there is a serpent who lies in wait, his focus is set on its next victim as he calculates his move. Let's take a look at what this looked like for Eve in Genesis chapter 3.

The serpent asks Eve:

"Has God indeed said, 'You shall not eat of every tree of the garden'?"

Eve responds to the serpent in verses 2 and 3:

2 ...we may eat the fruit of the trees of the garden;

3 but of the fruit of the tree which is in the midst of the garden, God has said, 'You shall not eat it, nor shall you touch it, lest you die.'"

As innocent as her statement appears to be on the surface, she misquoted God. Her version was more of a paraphrase. In doing this, she added to God's instructions. Her response lacked conviction and assurance. The words she spoke were not exactly the same words God spoke to Adam in the Garden. If anyone noticed her

CHAPTER 4 | TRIED AND TRUE

mistake, it was Satan. Despite Eve's desire to obey God's instructions, she erred in her account of the reason for her obedience. Let's compare Eve's interpretation of what God said with what He actually instructed.

Eve said in Genesis 3:2-3:

> *2 We may eat the fruit of the trees of the garden;*
>
> *3* ***but of the fruit of the tree, which is in the midst of the garden****, God has said, 'You shall not eat it,* ***nor shall you touch it****, lest you die.'"*

God said to Adam in Genesis 2:16-17:

> *"And the LORD God commanded the man, saying, "Of every tree of the garden you may freely eat; but of the* ***tree of the knowledge of good and evil*** *you shall not eat, for in the day that you eat of it you shall surely die."*

Eve's statement shows she knew the location of the forbidden tree, yet she did not have firsthand knowledge of the tree, as we see from her lack of familiarity with it. She referenced the tree by its location and not by its name. She said *"the tree that is in the midst of the garden."* This shows a level of uncertainty to the hearer; there is ambiguity in her statement. She quotes God, yet she added to His words. In the Bible, we read that

Eve is created after God gave the instructions concerning the tree. Therefore, it was Adam who would have had to share this information with Eve. She added to the instructions by saying that God said they *"shall not touch it."*

God never said that. I am uncertain of the depth of Eve's understanding of God's command. Whatever caused her to err in this way only paved the way for the adversary to come against her like a flood. He waited for her to be alone as she is his target. He would not have chosen Adam because Adam received the instructions directly from God. God gave dominion to Adam and made Eve his companion. Therefore, we presume that since Adam was in charge, he would have been the one to pass this information on to Eve. It is highly unlikely that Adam would fall for the devil's lies. It is my belief that Adam fell not because he was confused but because Eve fell first Adam would have to choose between his love for God and his love for Eve.

It was a smart move on Satan's part to target Eve first. Let us not place all of the blame on her because we weren't there and we really don't have that information made available to us. Perhaps Adam didn't exactly pass on the information to her verbatim, and that is why she misspoke. Perhaps she did not take it upon herself to seek

CHAPTER 4 | TRIED AND TRUE

clarification from God if she didn't completely understand. These things we will never know, but what we do know is that Eve's mistake gave the enemy a much-needed platform to get a foothold in. After he had her attention, he corrected her by imputing his version of what would happen if she were to eat of the fruit. Genesis 3:4-5 continues:

> *4 Then the serpent said to the woman, "You will not surely die.*
>
> *5 For God knows that in the day you eat of it your eyes will be opened, and you will be like God, knowing good and evil."*

Verse 6 shows us a blueprint of how Eve seamlessly completes the cycle of temptation in three easy steps:

> *6 "So, when the woman saw that the tree was good for food"*

- Lust of the flesh: the focus is on satisfying the instinctual desire to supply the body with nourishment for the sake of survival.

> *"that it was pleasant to the eyes,"*

- Lust of the eyes: the fruit appealed to her desires; it was appetizing. This is also instinctual, as we are more likely to eat something that looks good enough to eat.

> *"and a tree desirable to make one wise,"*

- The pride of life: it awakened an innate desire of self-edification, self-reliance, power, and independence; she would be like God.

"and she took of its fruit and ate."

- Marks the completion of the temptation, as she completed the cycle and immediately fell into sin.

Adam's fall is not outlined in this way. The Bible simply says that Eve gave Adam of the fruit, and he ate. The process of his decision is not illustrated. Perhaps it was an intentional omission to illustrate the willfulness of his decision. If I had to guess, the temptation for him was not the fruit, but Eve herself. Perhaps Adam reflected on when she was not there and was reminded of his loneliness. Perhaps he could discern that since she ate of the fruit, she would cease to exist to him. Maybe the idea of being alone was too much for him to bear. As the Word does not depict his thought process in its entirety, it is not useful to speculate. Instead, let's look at the second Adam and how He fared against this same cycle of temptation. Jesus is the second Adam.

Matthew 4 begins by giving us a glimpse into the physical condition of Jesus. He had fasted for 40 days and 40 nights; His body was weak and

CHAPTER 4 | TRIED AND TRUE

lacked physical sustenance. The Bible says Jesus was feeling the effects of the fast, because it says he was hungry. In Matthew 4:3, we see that Satan sticks to his modus operandi (M.O.) and begins the process with a question. This time, it is casting doubt on the identity of Jesus. It says:

> *"If You are the Son of God, command that these stones become bread."*

- Lust of the flesh: to fulfill a natural desire. In this case, it is hunger.

Jesus responds in verse 4:

> *"It is written, 'MAN SHALL NOT LIVE BY BREAD ALONE, BUT BY EVERY WORD THAT PROCEEDS FROM THE MOUTH OF GOD.'"*

Satan proceeds in verses 5-6:

> *5 "Then the devil took Him up into the holy city, set Him on the pinnacle of the temple,*
>
> *6 and said to Him, "If You are the Son of God, throw Yourself down. For it is written: 'HE SHALL GIVE HIS ANGELS CHARGE OVER YOU,' and, IN THEIR HANDS THEY SHALL BEAR YOU UP, LEST YOU DASH YOUR FOOT AGAINST A STONE.'"*

- Pride of Life: Jesus would gain personal glory in the assurance that God would protect the Messiah as written in Psalm 91. It is an attack on the image of Jesus as the Son of God.

Jesus responds in verse 7:

> *"It is written again, 'YOU SHALL NOT TEMPT THE LORD YOUR GOD.'"*

Satan, relentless in his pursuit, continues the temptation in verses 8-9:

> *8 "Again, the devil took Him up on an exceedingly high mountain and showed Him all the kingdoms of the world and their glory.*
>
> *9 And he said to Him, "All these things I will give You if You will fall down and worship me.""*

- Lust of the Eyes: Satan offers Jesus status and control over the kingdoms of the world.

Jesus replies in verse 10:

> *"Away with you, Satan! For it is written, 'YOU SHALL WORSHIP THE LORD YOUR GOD, AND HIM ONLY YOU SHALL SERVE.'"*

CHAPTER 4 | TRIED AND TRUE

- Jesus completed the cycle of temptation and triumphed over the enemy. Afterwards, the angels came and ministered to the Lord. Other versions read that the angels "attended" to the Lord.

Eve and Jesus underwent a complete cycle of temptation, although not in the same order. (Note: Luke's account of Jesus' temptations mirrors the same order as Eve's.) You can expect that the enemy will do the same to you. The difference between Eve and Jesus is that Jesus stood firm on the Word of God, whereas Eve gave the enemy her version of God's instructions. In Chapter 6 in the book of Ephesians, we learn that the Word is our Spiritual Sword (more on this in Chapter 6). If we do not use our sword in battle we will also fall into temptation and give in to sin.

We need to know the Word of God so we can wield it against the enemy when he attacks. Notice that when the enemy speaks, he gives his interpretation of the Word, which is rooted in lies. He twists the Word of God to confuse us. If you based your knowledge of the Word of God solely on the few verses spoken from the platforms of churches during weekly services, know that you are ill-equipped and will have more losses than wins against the daily battles of the enemy. You do not have to memorize it all at once, you just have to get it into your spirit at least once then the Holy

Spirit will remind you of the Word when you are faced with the devil's schemes.

In summary:

- Lust of the Flesh, in its simplest form, is any temptation that appeals to our senses to meet a basic need or gratify a natural desire without reliance on God to supply for it.

- Lust of the Eyes concerns superficial matters (i.e. social status, material gains, wealth, fame, etc.).
- Pride of Life includes achieving personal gains, the ego, pursuing glory, self-exaltation or accolades. The pursuit of these is sinful if we do it in disregard of God's perfect will.

Now, let's see how these three steps unfold in Satan's use of his atomic bomb: unforgiveness.

In Matthew, Chapter 6, Jesus teaches us to pray the prayer we now call "Our Father." For some of us, this prayer is the very first one learned as a child. Most of you are probably reciting the verses in your minds subconsciously as you read this text. In verse 12 of the Prayer, we ask God to forgive us our debts as we forgive our debtors.

CHAPTER 4 | TRIED AND TRUE

Other versions read "forgive us our trespasses as we forgive those who trespass against us." Forgiveness is vital, especially if Jesus saw it fit to include in our prayers. Not only did He include it in the original prayer to be followed, but then in verses 14 and 15, He expands on the subject. He says:

> *14 For if you forgive men their trespasses, your heavenly Father will also forgive you.*
>
> *15 But if you do not forgive men their trespasses, neither will your Father forgive your trespasses.*

Jesus is making sure the disciples understand that above all the requests you make before God in prayer, one should fully understand the importance of forgiveness and reconciliation. You should always seek to forgive others before expecting God to forgive you. In fact, in Matthew 5:22—24, Jesus says if you recall a contention with another as you present your gift to the Lord, then you are to reconcile before offering your gift unto God. Reconciliation and forgiveness are of vast importance to Him, and we should not take it lightly.

Among all the weapons of the enemy, Unforgiveness is his atomic bomb. It is the weapon that can completely wipe out humanity. It hardens your heart and, if left untreated, will lead to perdition. Unforgiveness is his specialty because he is on the receiving end of it. He is the only created thing that will never be forgiven because of his own rebellion against God. Think about it. You and I have sinned and so has the devil, yet you and I receive forgiveness and redemption through the blood of Jesus Christ and the devil does not—he is unforgiven. He achieves his level of expertise by routinely putting this weapon into action in the lives of men and women alike.

He has taken unforgiveness to a whole new level and through this mastery, he orchestrates events in our lives that cause, amongst other things, division, grief, strife, and loss. Offense works hand-in-hand with unforgiveness, and it is through the act of offense that one decides not to forgive. Once we have made up our minds to withhold forgiveness, then our decision seals our fate. No matter how active you are in the church or how many people you lead to Christ, if there is an unforgiving spirit within you, then you are among those the Lord speaks of in Matthew 7:21-23, where the Lord will say, "I never knew you—depart from me."

There was a man in a parable spoken by Jesus and recorded in the book of Matthew, Chapter 18, verses 21-35. This man owed the king ten thousand talents. That is the equivalent of

CHAPTER 4 | TRIED AND TRUE

approximately $14 billion dollars by today's standards. The king desired to settle his outstanding accounts, and the man did not have the funds to repay what he owed. Therefore, the king ordered to have the man, along with his wife, children, and all that belonged to him to be sold in order to get payment on his debt. The man begged the king for patience so he could get the money he needed to repay the king.

The Bible says it moved the king with compassion and therefore he released the man from captivity and forgave the debt. Upon the man's release, the man found another man, one of his debtors, who owed him 100 denarii. That is equivalent to a little under $12 thousand dollars today. The Bible says that this man laid hands on the debtor, but it wasn't to pray! He grabbed the debtor by the throat and demanded repayment. The debtor makes the same request the man had made before the king. The debtor asks the man to have patience with him, that he would soon repay. However, the man was unmoved.

He would not forgive his debtor, although the king forgave him. To make matters worse, the man imprisoned the debtor until the debt was settled. Those who witnessed the event went back and shared news of this with the king. He became angry with the man because he should have acted with the same forgiveness and compassion he had just been afforded. Therefore, the king turned the man over to torturers until he could repay his original $14 billion-dollar debt. The story concludes with a warning from Jesus in verse 35:

> *"So [will] My heavenly Father also will do to you if each of you, from his heart, does not forgive his brother his trespasses."*

That is why unforgiveness is an effective weapon for the enemy. It works because it is easy to fall into without knowing it. Unforgiveness is the doorman to hell. There was a time when I struggled with unforgiveness, and I had to come to God and surrender my will for His before I could forgive. I did not know how to forgive but I knew if I did not, then God would not forgive me. He has made that abundantly clear. I was not about to let a person, who let themselves be used and blinded by the devil, prevent me from living the life God designed for me here on Earth and in Heaven.

One thing about unforgiveness is that when someone hurts you, the transgression is a wound against you, your pride, and ego. No matter how much you pretend to be humble and unaffected by pride and ego, the moment offense creeps in, they rear their ugly little heads. The "self" is not too far behind, as it serves as a sounding board for not forgiving someone. The moment forgiveness enters your mind, shortly thereafter, the devil inserts

CHAPTER 4 | TRIED AND TRUE

questionable thoughts also as he begins the cycle of temptation with unforgiveness as the end goal in mind. In the case of Eve vs. the serpent, the devil's first question was aimed at attacking the Word of God. He starts with *"Has God indeed said....?"* In the case of Jesus vs. Satan, the devil's first raised question was aimed at Jesus' identity. He started that round with *"If you are the Son of God..."* In the case of **you** vs. Satan, the devil begins his cycle with "Is it necessary for you to forgive such-and-such or so-and-so?"

Remember, as we discussed earlier:

- *Lust of the Flesh*: any temptation that appeals to our senses to meet a basic need or gratify a natural desire in a way that satisfies the need without reliance on God.
- *Lust of the Eyes*: superficial matters (i.e. social status, material gains, wealth, fame, etc.)
- *Pride of Life*: achieving personal gains, the ego, the pursuit of glory, self-exaltation, or accolades. The pursuit of these is sinful if we do it in disregard of God's perfect will.

In the case of you vs. Satan, below are the responses one might give as we face unforgiveness:

The lust of the flesh may appeal to survival instincts. Therefore, your response to the question "How will forgiving affect me?" may be:

"If this person gets away with that, then he/she will always do this to me, and I will be exposed to harm and hurt continually. How can I survive like that?"

The lust of the eyes may appeal to the person's image and social status:

"If I forgive this person, then what will others think of me? Then, "others" might do the same or view me differently altogether.

The pride of life tempts you to esteem yourself as more important than others:

"It is not fair for me to suffer all the time. When will people finally consider me? No, I will not forgive, and to prevent this from happening again, I will take matters into my own hands and the next person who tries something like this will pay for it dearly. To make sure this does not happen again, I will treat everyone differently from now on. I will be less trusting to protect my interests."

The pride of life is the gateway to a never-ending cycle. I know a woman who was hurt by her previous husband. She was a loving, loyal, and very giving wife in her marriage. Her husband did not reciprocate in kind. Therefore, they were soon divorced. This experience left her very hurt and scarred. She never became close again with

CHAPTER 4 | TRIED AND TRUE

anyone else. She lived a very promiscuous life thereafter and traveled from place to place looking for a way to drown out the emptiness she felt inside. She began to drink to drown out her pain and soon she frequented bars and clubs regularly to justify her precarious behavior. Surprisingly enough, she remarried after living a life that would make any contestant on the bachelorette or bachelor blush. Remembering how harshly she was treated in her previous marriage, she would no longer cook for her mate as an expression of love and she would make him cook daily, instead. Since her husband worked late nights, she would force him to prepare dinner before he left to work, no matter the time.

She did not demand it of him, but in a very manipulative and cunning way, she would lead her husband to believe it was his duty. Despite all his efforts to please his wife, she was always cold and angry with mostly everyone around. She was miserable and, soon enough, the wife faced another divorce. Both parties left in a bitter and cold state. Not only did the cycle of unforgiveness start all over again, but it produced two contestants from the one.

Jesus talked about the importance of forgiveness. The way to find it within is to first learn how to die to yourself daily. Dying to self is the key that unlocks the ability to forgive wholeheartedly. When the opportunity to forgive arises, always forgive from your heart. Forgiveness means that you also forget and don't bring up the matter every chance you get. If you did, then you would not be a child of God who forgives; you would be a creature created by God who accuses. If you regularly accuse your brethren, then what is the difference between you and the one our Bible calls the accuser? Do not become an instrument of the devil by yielding to the desire to hold a grudge and withhold forgiveness from those who have created an offense against you. I read somewhere that holding onto a grudge (or holding onto feelings of resentment and anger) is like holding onto a piece of burning coal, intending to throw it at someone else to harm them. However, you only harm yourself, because it is your hand that ultimately gets burnt.

When debating on whether to forgive, remember this: your life is no longer your own, it is hidden in Christ's life. Therefore, it is no longer you who lives, but Christ who lives within you (Galatians 2:20). If Christ lives in you, then do what Jesus would do. When faced with the opportunity to forgive someone undeserving of it, He forgives. We see this example in Luke 23:34, where He asks God the Father to forgive those who encouraged His crucifixion. Do not forget that God also forgave us by the blood of Jesus even when we ourselves do not deserve forgiveness. Therefore,

CHAPTER 4 | TRIED AND TRUE

when faced with the decision to forgive, choose wholehearted forgiveness. When I completely surrendered myself to God, I decided to live in complete surrender to His Word. When I believe Galatians 2:20, forgiveness is easier to do because I have now removed my "self" from the equation.

Unforgiveness is a gateway for the enemy to open the floodgates against you. It leads to bitterness, regret, and resentment. All these kill your joy, destroy vision, and lead to physical illnesses that cannot be cured, and it prevents healing from taking place. This is because there is no room for physical healing when you need an emotional healing instead. Most diseases come from the body's inability to rest. You cannot enter God's rest with a spirit of unforgiveness. I could not walk into this new season of my life as long as I held resentment in my heart after suffering from "church-hurt." I had to wholeheartedly forgive those who hurt me so I could receive the blessings of God. After I forgave, it was like the floodgates of heaven descended upon me and I began to experience blessing after blessing. My prayers were answered with increasing frequency and I experienced joy, peace, and happiness. If you have ever experienced church-hurt, remember that those who hurt you are just as imperfect as you are and make mistakes, too. Adversity builds character, so chalk it up to character-building experiences.

STEAL, KILL & DESTROY

My "church-hurt" experience was a character-building one. I learned how to be more discerning and to truly wait upon the instructions of the Lord. God also sent Jesus to die for them on the Cross; they are my brothers and sisters in Christ. When I place people, places, or ideas on the throne of my life, a place that belongs to God alone, then I unwittingly pave the way for the enemy to use those very things that I hold in high regard as a weapon against me. Those very things will be used as deterrents from God's purpose and perfect will for my life.

Do not let the same afflictions delay the blessings that God has for you. Do not give the enemy any more weapons to use against you. Disarm the enemy today and prevent him from using these weapons by doing frequent checks of the heart. Heart checks will reveal your true motives for doing things. Are you doing them for God or because the church *needs* you. How does it make you feel to know that you are *needed?* Be careful because what starts out as a sincere desire to be helpful could easily transform into an ego booster or a temporary fix to a much deeper void. Even little things such as serving in the church can become idols in our lives if they take the place of God. Ask the Holy Spirit to inspect your heart and its motives regularly. The Holy Spirit is faithful and knows your heart better than you.

Another weapon that stagnates spiritual growth is fear. Second Timothy 1:7 (NKJV) says:

> "... God has not given us a spirit of fear, but of power and of love and of a sound mind."

Fear is of the enemy. It keeps us captive to ideas that are not even real. These ideas are just perceived threats, not actual ones. The Lord has given us natural fears that help preserve our lives—I am not speaking of these. I am speaking of the paralyzing fears that prevent us from walking on the path the Lord has faithfully laid out before us. The devil uses fear to control us and to carry out his agenda. The devil is a terrorist! It has been my observation that he uses fears to prevent people from receiving the blessings and promises of God. This also affects healing. Sometimes people have received negative reports from doctors and fear (amongst other things) prevents some people from receiving healing. Now, this is not an all-inclusive statement. There are other barriers to healing. However, fear ranks high on that list, second only to unforgiveness.

The enemy is running short on time and is taking the gloves off. He is pulling out all the stops to ensure he is successful in these last days. The Bible says in Revelation 12:12 that the enemy has great wrath because he knows his time is short. I do not expect him to play nice at all, especially against us who have an assignment by God to win souls by spreading the Gospel. Jesus commands in Matthew 28:19-20 (NKJV) to:

> *19 "Go therefore and make disciples of all the nations, baptizing them in the name of the Father and of the Son and of the Holy Spirit,*
>
> *20 teaching them to observe all things that I have commanded you; and lo, I am with you always, even to the end of the age." Amen.*

We have our assignment and the enemy has his. His success rests on his ability to keep us from the knowledge of God's plans for our lives. He does this by trying to sever our relationship with God. The best way to sever any relationship is to start by breaking down the communication. If he can control the narrative, then he can dictate the outcome. That is his goal. By doing this, he controls the information you receive, preventing you from uncovering truths in the Word of God.

If he is successful, you eventually go from reading the Word daily, to only when you're having bad days, to only during Sunday services, etc. No

CHAPTER 4 | TRIED AND TRUE

need to bring your Bibles to church on Sundays, the Word is projected for you during service. If you don't know the Word for yourself, it is easy for confusion to creep in and to believe false indoctrination because it "sounds" like the Word. It will be like when the serpent caused Eve to become confused about what God really said. The further away you are from the Word of God, the easier it is for the enemy to fool you into believing a characteristic of God that is not like Him at all.

After all is said and done, you will find that *you* are the enemy's biggest weapon. I once heard a public speaker say that our biggest enemy is the "in-ner-me." However, it does not have to be so. The number one way to disarm the enemy and take away the weapon of *you* from him is to pick up your Bible and read the Word. It is the first step to winning battles against the adversary.

CHAPTER 5 | B.C. MOMENTS

So shall they fear The name of the LORD from the west, And His glory from the rising of the sun; When the enemy comes in like a flood, The Spirit of the LORD will lift up a standard against him.

Isaiah 59:19 (NKJV)

Before Christ (B.C.) moments are moments I reflect on today as a way to measure my current level of spiritual growth from where I once was. A B.C. moment is any behavior or attribute that surfaces during a time of testing that is not godly. These attributes for me are: lack of patience, anger that can easily transform into a rage, self-reliance, profanity, and unforgiveness. The one I most fell into time and time again was anger. I have to say, anger is one that took longer to heal from than the others.

CHAPTER 5 | B.C. MOMENTS

While I do not feel as if I have "arrived", I am not where I used to be.

I have gotten better at identifying these moments as they come, and I have been able to respond in a more God-like manner in comparison to when I'm in B.C. mode. It is a constant renewing of the mind through the washing of the Word of God that raises the standard of what an appropriate response is for those moments. I don't want to do what is right because it is right; instead, I desire to do what is right because I desire to be more and more Christlike. Another challenge has always been my response to my children's negative behaviors.

Most children enter rebellious phases during their teenage years. I gave my life to Christ when my daughter was in high school. I used to joke that it was her high school years that brought me closer to God. I have to say, those years were the most trying because while I was trying to instill a good sense of morals and values from a biblical perspective, there was an entire world enticing children to do otherwise. This experience taught me that it is ideal to be in Christ first, and then get married and have children.

Ideally, it would be nice to encounter God at a young age so that by the time you are in early adulthood, you can have a solid foundation in place as a result of a close relationship with God. This way, you can rest on that strong foundation as you navigate through the challenges this life brings. You can draw from the knowledge of the Word instilled in you without having to consult with your parents. After you reach maturity and have married your second-to-God, then children can come into play; but not too soon, all in God's timing. In the Old Testament, newlywed husbands could not go to war, as it was necessary for them to stay with their brides for at least a year. This is sound counsel even today. A year is just enough time to ensure you get to know each other and learn to function as one body.

After you have settled into your marriage, then you can focus your attention on building a family. All the wisdom you gained prior to this point, you can now share with your family so they too can benefit from a solid foundation. If any of these is out of order, you will face more challenges than necessary. God is a God of order; it is important that we follow His principles and teachings regarding daily living. This way, we pave the way for those who come behind us. This is the ideal scenario however this is not how it played out for me. I lived life outside of the will of God and my early family building years were governed by worldly views. Our family struggled amidst the chaos after I gave my life to God and we tried to correct the blueprint for living amidst a sinful world. Everything we once thought was right wasn't, and so the transition from an ungodly worldview to a Godly one was bumpy. Praise God for His grace and mercy. God restores and has made our family whole through the washing and renewing of our minds. If you missed it like I did, no worries, God restores and makes things whole again. All you have to do is repent and completely surrender to His will and His desires. Step aside and let God do the work and you will see how much better life will be.

By the time our family made it through the high school years we reached a level of maturity in Christ that truly embodies the truth of Philippians 4:13. I find it interesting how many people take that verse completely out of context. While it is empowering to think you can do all things through Christ who strengthens you, let us back up a few verses and see what Paul is really saying here. In verse 11, in response to the provision sent to him by the Philippians, he says:

> "... I have learned in whatever state I am, to be content:"

Try this the next time you get a negative report from your child's school.

Paul continues to emphasize his experience in verse 12:

> *"I know how to be abased, and I know how to abound. Everywhere and in all things, I have learned both to be full and to be hungry, both to abound and to suffer need."*

He concludes in verse 13 with the reason behind his ability to endure:

> *"I can do all things through Christ who strengthens me."*

I remember the aha moment I experienced when I understood this verse in its context. Surely, yes, we can do all things through Christ who strengthens us, but I am sure Paul was referring to his ability to endure all things through the strength that God so willingly provides. Paul understood that God's power is best experienced during his moments of weakness. He said that God's power is made perfect in his weaknesses (Second Corinthians 12:9 NKJV). Paul did not have a problem surrendering his will for God's as he understood the benefit is Victory in Christ through all adversity. It is a moment of victory when you reach a level of maturity in your walk

CHAPTER 5 | B.C. MOMENTS

with Christ where surrendering your will for God's becomes second nature. Thereafter, no matter what you face, you will have peace *and* you will overcome. You will truly experience the peace that surpasses all understanding. When my daughter graduated from high school, it was Philippians 4:13 that she willingly wrote on her cap! That was God's way of telling me she was not the only one graduating that day. If you as a parent can survive your child's high school years, then, indeed, you really *can* do all things through Christ who strengthens you.

I know what God expects of me. He has strengthened me to endure and overcome through the power of the blood of Jesus and His Holy Word. I can no longer blame my upbringing, my race, the neighborhood I grew up in, or even my economic status to justify behavior outside of the character of God. I did not follow the "ideal pathway" to forming a family, because my family building days were all B.C. This doesn't mean I cannot set the example for my children and set a standard for them based on biblical teachings. As I write this book, my pastor, Jamie Jones, is finishing up a series on consecration. Last Sunday, he said that you "have to decide that *generational* sin stops with you."

I've decided to be the difference in my ancestral lineage. It is no longer acceptable to say you live a certain way or do things a certain way because that is how your parents did it. First Peter 2:9 says we are a chosen generation and in it we are called "a royal priesthood." In Ephesians 2:10, Paul says we are God's handiwork, which He created in Christ for good works prepared in advance for us to do. This means we have a purpose. We are here by design and God is the Creator. Therefore, living life by His design allows you to receive the most benefit and blessings now in real time, not just in Heaven.

In life, we will have challenges. However, Jesus has overcome them all. A. W. Tozer, in his book, *The Attributes of God*, expresses many times to the reader that God has already lived all of our tomorrows (Tozer, 2007). Jesus says in John 16:33 (NKJV):

> *"These things I have spoken to you, that in Me you may have peace. In the world you will have tribulation; but be of good cheer, I have overcome the world."*

What this verse tells me is that in Jesus, I have peace despite the trouble the world may bring. This verse is the reason I should no longer experience B.C. Moments. Those are horrible and leave me feeling empty and defeated. Most of all, I

CHAPTER 5 | B.C. MOMENTS

feel disgusted, because it is no longer a character I can relate with. B.C. Moments are uncomfortable for me, and I declare I no longer have these, thanks to the grace and love of Jesus Christ and Holy Spirit who is instrumental in these moments.

In B.C. mode, outbursts were normal for me. Yet, the closer I got to Jesus, the more conviction I would receive from Holy Spirit right after one of these moments. Holy Spirit would replay the incident in my mind in the same way that a coach does with his team. The coach goes over past games and offers alternative plays to help improve performance; he raises the standard to achieve a win the next time you get to play. Similarly, Holy Spirit led me and showed me the areas where there is much room for improvement. At the height of the incidents, I would be knee-deep in anger. I would become infuriated and immediately resort to yelling. With enough coaching sessions, eventually got to where I could no longer even raise my voice in anger. I would be immediately convicted afterwards, as it did not seem like an appropriate response.

With my daughter, it was rawer and more emotional. Holy Spirit was gentle in His leading and gave me a bird's-eye view of the situation at hand. I could see that I was outside of the will of God with my response more than whatever caused my anger. Imagine an upset child mid-tantrum that yells out, *"Fine!"* in response to whatever was egging him or her on; that was me. At first conviction, I did not want to yield, because I wanted to get my point across. Soon, I started to really hear what God was telling me in that moment, and when I felt I was about to lose it, my response changed to, "This isn't right and we are going to pray about this *right now*!"

By resorting to prayer whenever conflict would arise, my response disarmed the enemy and he could no longer use it to make me stumble. Instead, the conflict was building my faith and my reliance on God to handle the situation. I presented the matter to Him and left it there. I would always pray for God to shed light on the situation and to bring understanding and healing to the areas that needed it so that this would not happen again. I would pray the Scriptures that touched on the subject or dealt with whatever the issue was so as to bring correction to not only my daughter but also to myself as a mother in my response.

I can laugh about it now as I reflect, because I don't recognize the B.C. version of me. I will be honest though; in the middle of those moments, it is so hard to keep it together when you are not

CHAPTER 5 | B.C. MOMENTS

walking in the Spirit. It did not take long for me to realize that in the heat of these moments, the best thing to do is to make a conscious decision to put God at the center. Chip Ingram has a book called *Overcoming Emotions that Destroy* and in it, he says anger is a secondary emotion (Ingram, Johnson, 2015). And he is correct. I was angry because I was afraid. I feared losing my daughter to such an unforgiving world. I did not have Chip's book at the time to guide me; all I had was Holy Spirit. After each session, Holy Spirit led me to dig deeper to what was really at the core of my anger. In the end, I surrendered. I remember that when I came back to God, I went into a season of constant prayer and intercession. Sometimes, I would feel the leading of Holy Spirit waking me up to pray.

One morning, I got up to pray very early. The B.C. Moments were frequent, and I felt as if the enemy was using them to draw a wedge between my daughter and I. That morning, the sun wasn't even out yet. It must have been around 5am when I surrendered my daughter to God. I released my hold on her and the control I thought I had over her to God. I realized that before she was mine, she was His. He doesn't want her to go down the wrong path any more than I do. He has more power than I can to ensure she is safe. In comparison, I can do nothing; but God can do it all. Sure, yes, she has free will, but I know that every time someone has an encounter with God, a true encounter, there is no turning back from His love. I believe that when the Maldonado's came to Christ, we did so as a family and it was a true God-encounter.

So, I began to pray differently. Although not verbatim, my prayers for her would go something like this:

"Lord, let my child's life be filled with God-encounters. Ignite in her a passion to seek You every day. Let her desire to live a life that is pleasing to Your eyes. God, surround her with positive influences and keep her from the negative ones. Bless every aspect of her being and all of her endeavors. Bless her goings and her comings. Father, may she be a mighty woman of God and, most of all, make her a worthy vessel of honor to carry forth the Gospel to the lost. May she be a true example of what it means to have a relationship with you, and may all her actions reflect your mark upon her life. In the mighty name of Jesus Christ, I pray, amen."

As I yield my control and completely surrender my will for her life to God, I continued to pray this way for her and still do, though she is older and more mature now. One morning as I

CHAPTER 5 | B.C. MOMENTS

prayed, she entered my room. It was still dark, but I could see her standing at my bedroom door. She could see I was on my knees and praying. I asked if she was okay and asked her why she was up hours before she had to wake up for school. Her response to me was "Mommy, I think God wants me to pray with you," and we did. Yielding control is something that I have to do frequently because of my nature to want the best for my child and to lead but there is no greater leader than God and I do not love her more than He does. In this story it is Holy Spirit who is the real MVP. He is the one who leads me and guides me. Although it is not always pretty or easy it is always what's best for that moment.

Amid B.C. Moments, you lose peace. God is not the author of confusion. If you are in a "passionate" discussion and no one is getting their point across, invite Holy Spirit into that situation and watch how things change. Most of my B.C. Moments were because of undue stress and fear that things were getting out of control. I was a fool to believe this. God is always in control. Now, I hold fast to the promises of the Lord. I made the statement told to a jailer in the Bible my own. When the jailer fell before Paul and Silas and asked what he must do to be saved, they replied as Acts 16:31 (NKJV) says:

STEAL, KILL & DESTROY

...*"Believe on the Lord Jesus Christ, and you will be saved, you and your household."*

Now, here am I, the pot calling the kettle black while I call out the believer who takes Scripture out of context. I know the above verse's meaning. I have the "head" knowledge that what is meant in this verse is that since the jailer felt the conviction of sin, repented and believed, in like manner, his household will [also need to do in order to] be saved. However, there is nothing wrong with believing that God will bring salvation to my household the way He brought salvation unto the jailer.

My daughter is beyond the years of accountability, therefore, her repentance and responsibility of accountability for her walk with God falls on her. I cannot do it for her, but I can continue to point her back to God. If she should stumble and fall, I will still love her unconditionally and trust that He who started a good work in her is faithful to complete it. I never cease to pray, because prayer moves mountains and they also rid you of BC Moments.

CHAPTER 6 | THE WEAPONS OF OUR WARFARE

"For the weapons of our warfare are not carnal but mighty in God for pulling down strongholds,"
2 Corinthians 10:4

I remember when I came back to the Lord, He ignited in me a passion and desire to seek Him more through prayer, intercession, and through the growth and knowledge of His Word. The Bible instructs us to grow in the grace and knowledge of God (2 Peter 3:18). The most practical way to do this is by connecting with His Word daily. The Word of God is vital to our success in this walk. If you are lacking in faith, may I prescribe to you the Word of God?

Scripture says faith comes by hearing and hearing through the Word of God (Romans 10:17).

CHAPTER 6 | THE WEAPONS OF OUR WARFARE

If you are suffering an illness, may I prescribe to you the Word of God? Isaiah 53:5 says that by His stripes, we are healed. You don't have to be an English teacher to know that the word "healed" is written in the past tense in Scripture. Isaiah prophesied about the healing power of Jesus 700 years before His birth and still wrote it in the past tense.

God is very intentional in all He does. I believe Isaiah spoke of the healing power of Jesus before He came on the scene because God stands outside of time. When He says "it is done", then it is—even if it hasn't manifested in our realm yet. Every problem that plagues mankind, you can rest assured that in 99 out of 100 problems, the problem is a byproduct of *our* sins. God deals with the problem of sin and teaches us through Scripture how to live practical Christian lives here on Earth filled with purpose and the manifestations of the power and promises of God. Powerful things happen when you apply the Word of God to your daily life. The Word of God is living and active, and therefore it is constantly speaking to our current situation. The Bible is not just an ancient book; it is the basis for living today.

STEAL, KILL & DESTROY

Before we dive into the weapons of our warfare, I cannot stress enough the importance of connecting with the Word of God daily. Without it, we are ill-equipped for this battle against the powers of darkness. In Psalm 119:105, we learn that His word is a lamp to our feet and a light onto our path. Most individuals go their entire lives without discovering what their purpose is or in which direction they should go when all they need to do is to connect with the Word of God.

When mobile devices and apps became popular back in the day, there was an advertising campaign that coined the term "There's an app for that!" Well, just so you know, there is a Bible verse for every situation you may encounter in this walk. There's a verse for that! There isn't a single aspect of your life that God has not already seen and/or hasn't planned for. The most surprising thing to me is that whenever I am at my lowest and God seems far from me, the moment I pick up my Bible, it immediately bridges the gap. I feel at peace and refreshed every time. Rest in the assurance that no matter what you may face in this life, God has it covered.

CHAPTER 6 | THE WEAPONS OF OUR WARFARE

Jesus said in John 10:27 that His sheep know His voice and He knows them. This connection requires a level of intimacy that goes higher than a casual Sunday Bible reading session. There is no better way to know someone's character than by drawing from actual examples and real-life experiences. The Bible does just that. When you read the Word, God's character comes to life!

With the knowledge of God's character, it changes your testimony of Him. It transforms your life as you become an imitator of His character. Suddenly, you are more than a conqueror! Conquerors defeat! The Word of God says in Revelation 12:11 that the enemy is defeated by the power of the blood of the Lamb and the power of their testimony (referring to the saints). Faith comes by hearing and hearing by the Word of God. As your knowledge of the Word of God grows, so does your faith. When you hear of the big miracles God performed, you believe Him for bigger miracles in your own life; miracles you will testify of for the glory of God.

The Word of God is one big testimony of Jesus and of God's redemptive power. Through the Word, God shares His character with us. We experience it through the stories shared in the sacred text. This is how God communicates with us. Reading the Bible is like reading God's diary. It is a window peering into the heart of God.

The Bible says in Luke 6:45 that the mouth speaks what the heart is full of. There is power in the Word of God. When you become full of His Word, it fills you with power. The Word of God renews our minds and through it, we gain understanding. God communicates through His Word while we communicate with God through prayer. Some of us feel awkward in prayer, not because we don't know how to pray or because we don't like it, but because we lack in the knowledge of God's Word, so we do not hear Him speaking back. Therefore, our prayers become sessions of one-sided conversations with the walls in the room we are in. One-sided conversations are weird. Eventually, we get tired and cut the prayer time down. We talk and talk and talk and when we don't hear from God, we end with an "amen" and move on. This is not the way God intended our prayer lives to be.

CHAPTER 6 | THE WEAPONS OF OUR WARFARE

God desires us to have a meaningful conversation with Him in the same way you share meaningful conversations with your spouse or even a best friend. There are some people in my life that I can talk to for hours. My sister-in-law is one of them. I know that when we get on the phone, chances are, it will be awhile before we get off. Some would say it is because we don't speak as often as we used to, but that is not so. Even when we were neighbors, before we became sisters-in-law, our conversations were meaningful, because she has a pretty good idea of who I am and I have a pretty good idea of who she is. Sure, people change, but God is unchanging. The way to get to know God is through His Word. Without it, you are at a loss.

God cares about you and, through prayer, you can grow your relationship with Him. Some have said to me that they do not know how to pray. Recently, an elderly woman shared this with me. I was shocked to hear it, because she is a woman who has been in the church most of her life. However, she confided in me that she did not know how to pray. So, I showed her how by praying with her. I did not quote Scripture although it fuels prayer, nor did I say anything too deep for her understanding. My prayer is simple because all it is, is a conversation between my Father and me. I find that these prayers are answered quicker than others.

If you don't know what to say, talk about your day. I do. I tell God all about how annoying certain things were or the things I did not get done or wanted to do. I invite Him into my every day. In the nighttime, I share with Him my plans and ask for His assistance in giving me the time I need to get the tasks done. I asked God for time to finish writing this book and, suddenly, I get a week off from work, just like that.

If you don't know where to start, start by talking about your day. He cares about it—yes, even the small, menial parts. He wants you to share them with Him. It is true that He already knows, because He knows everything, but He is also your heavenly Father. If you as a parent delight in hearing all about your kids' day, even though you may know how it turned out, what makes you think God does not want to hear all about yours? He delights in you! Yes, you! When

CHAPTER 6 | THE WEAPONS OF OUR WARFARE

you trust God with your everyday, miracles will happen.

One thing that always moves me to tears is when I think about the greatness of God. He is so great, yet He is not so far-off or too great to miss the smallest details of my life. God has a way of making me feel like I am the only person in the world He cares about. I know this is not true, but He always makes me feel as if I am His favorite; you're His favorite, too! God cares about the things you care about.

I remember a time when I was working as a consultant. This role required me to travel on a weekly basis to the client site in Atlanta as part of a project that lasted about six months. I was growing weary and missed my family. Since I was alone in a city I did not know, every night when I went back to the hotel room, I would open up my Bible and simply read. I remember on one particular day becoming anxious about the safety of my children. It was an unreasonable fear, because my husband was home with them, and he is more than able to care for them. If I thought about this fear rationally, I would have identified this as an attack of the enemy with a purpose to afflict me with anxiety.

STEAL, KILL & DESTROY

Staying true to my routine, I read the Word of God. As I read First Samuel, Chapter 17, I got to the part where Jesse sent David with food to his brothers. David was a young shepherd and, while he was obedient to the desires of his father, he also loved his sheep. David spent most, if not all, of his time tending the sheep. He walked away from the thing he loved and enjoyed for the sake of obedience to his father. Menial as it may have been, out of the ordinary, an opportunity to be extraordinary arose. This errand opened the door to his triumph over Goliath. When I got to verse 20, it read:

> *"So, David rose early in the morning, left the sheep with a keeper, and took the things and went as Jesse had commended him..."*

At first, I read over these words quickly, but there was a quickening in my spirit that told me to go back. The words *left the sheep with a keeper* resonated with me. I read them aloud a few times before it hit me. He who guards over Israel is also

CHAPTER 6 | THE WEAPONS OF OUR WARFARE

keeping my children. My children are safe with Him. I wept.

The Lord thought enough of me to assure me that the anxious thoughts the enemy tried to flood my mind with were nothing but thoughts because He has my kids covered. While I love my children, I will never love them more than God loves them. They are safe in His hands. Without taking the time to read the Word of God, I would have been alone in that hotel room with anxious thoughts that would have plagued me. Those anxious thoughts are the fiery darts of the enemy.

After reading the passage, I understood that, as ordinary as my business trips to Atlanta may appear to be on the surface, God was doing something extraordinary behind the scenes. My job during that season was to seek intimacy with the Lord and to fill myself with His Word. God was strengthening me in Him for the plans He has for me. He was sharpening my sword and preparing me for battle.

God has given all Christians a spiritual armor to protect them during times of battle with the enemy. I am certain the Word of God, although it is the sword of the Spirit, is also the glue that sustains the armor and keeps it intact. During a time of anxious thoughts, it was the Word of God that reinforced my helmet of salvation. It protected my thoughts and replaced anxious thoughts with the reassurance of the power and sovereignty of God. It assured me of God's faithfulness, which disarmed the enemy's attack on my mind.

In this generation, one of the enemy's most successful tactics is to attack a person's mind. He fires his darts and aims them straight for your head. If he is successful, you will end up losing your mind. Working in social services as a Child Protective Investigator, I realized more and more that the Devil is attacking the minds of our youth and that of our mothers and fathers. This attack of the minds within this last generation should not come as a surprise to those who read the Word.

The Bible says in Deuteronomy 28:28 (NKJV) that a penalty for disobedience is madness. It reads, *"The LORD will strike you with madness and blindness and confusion of heart."* The devil cannot target you with a curse unless there is a basis for it. The Bible says in Proverbs 26:2 (NKJV) that *"Like a flitting sparrow, like a flying swallow,*

CHAPTER 6 | THE WEAPONS OF OUR WARFARE

So a curse without a cause shall not alight." In this generation, disobedience abounds, and rebellion has grabbed hold of many. There are plenty of reasons for this that I will not get into, however, it does not render us helpless. Paul instructs us in Ephesians 6:10-20 to put on the whole armor of God so we may stand against the wiles of the devil.

The armor of God comprises the belt of truth, the breastplate of righteousness, the shoes of peace, the shield of faith, the helmet of salvation and the sword of the spirit. Paul instructs us to put on the whole armor of God. It is vital for our success against the enemy today. I remember when I started this walk with God and would hear preachers refer to the armor of God, but they never really got into the practical aspect of how one goes about putting on the whole armor of God in their message. In theory, it sounds great, but how do you do that exactly?

I turned to elders in my church and all they could provide me with were theoretical applications on the subject. Someone said to me, "Well, in the morning, I imagine that I put on the armor of God as I put on my clothes and that is how I put on the armor of God." Seeing as I was not getting any closer to a revelation on this matter, I took it upon myself to write on a giant-sized Post-it® note Ephesians 6:11 through 18. I posted it on my wall right next to my dresser mirror. Every morning, I did not pretend to put on the armor of God, but I prayed daily as I looked at the verses.

While I got dressed, I would read over the verses while asking God to enlighten my understanding of this matter. I asked God to send me someone who has a full understanding of the armor of God so I may learn from them. Sometime later, I met an elderly woman. She carried one of those Bibles that was falling apart. She must have been around 70 or 80 years old and I just knew that anyone who carried a Bible that was falling apart lived a life that was put together. I befriended this lady and eventually asked her about the armor of God.

To my surprise, she did not have a practical application of these verses either. I was no wiser than when I first asked the question. I was so disappointed because I thought for sure, she would know the answer. I judged her level of

CHAPTER 6 | THE WEAPONS OF OUR WARFARE

knowledge based on the condition of her Bible. All I learned from this is that you can read your Bible all day long, but if you do not receive a revelation from Holy Spirit about what you are reading, you are no better off than the person who hasn't read the Word at all. My advice to you is to invite Holy Spirit to teach you the Word of God as you read it, so that you are truly receiving from it.

Finally, I searched on the internet for an answer and stumbled across Chip Ingram's book, *The Invisible War* (Ingram, 2015). I thank God for Chip and his obedience to God's calling on his life. His book helped me see what Paul meant when he commanded us to put on the whole armor of God. Before I give you my takeaway from Chip's book and the biblical text, let's first read Paul's instruction to the church. I pray that Holy Spirit enlightens your understanding in the same way He opened up this subject to me in Jesus' name.

Ephesians 6:10-18 reads:

10 Finally, my brethren, be strong in the Lord and in the power of His might.

11 Put on the whole armor of God, that you may be able to stand against the wiles of the devil.

12 For we do not wrestle against flesh and blood, but against principalities, against powers, against the rulers of the darkness of this age, against spiritual hosts of wickedness in the heavenly places.

13 Therefore, take up the whole armor of God, that you may be able to withstand in the evil day, and having done all, to stand.

14 Stand therefore, having girded your waist with truth, having put on the breastplate of righteousness,

15 and having shod your feet with the preparation of the gospel of peace;

16 above all, taking the shield of faith with which you will be able to quench all the fiery darts of the wicked one.

17 And take the helmet of salvation, and the sword of the Spirit, which is the word of God;

18 praying always with all prayer and supplication in the Spirit, being watchful to this end with all

CHAPTER 6 | THE WEAPONS OF OUR WARFARE

perseverance and supplication for all the saints..."

First, Paul instructs us to be strong in the Lord and in the power of His might. He says we must put on the whole armor of God. This means it is possible for you to think you are fully equipped with the entire armor of God but miss a piece or two. After reminding us to put on the whole armor of God, he reminds us of who our adversary is. In doing so, he assures us we are fighting a real war. He says more than once that after we have done all, to stand. I interpret this to mean that after you have come to the end of your own efforts, *stand, therefore, having girded your waist with truth.*

This seems like an odd thing to say until you read Chip Ingram's book. There, he explains that at the time of Paul's writing, he was in prison. While there, he observed the Roman soldiers and drew inspiration for this text through observation of their attire. He explains that the soldier's belt held together the entire armor. Likewise, as a Christian wearing the full armor of God, the belt of truth is your most important garment because it holds all your armor together. One "simple" lie can compromise your entire coat of armor, exposing you to the attack of the enemy, because you left that part of your life exposed.

    For instance, let's say your employer lets you enter your time on an electronic timecard instead of clocking in on a traditional system. One day, you get to work at 9:15am and you were supposed to be there at 9:00am. You are always punctual. However, on this morning, there was a bad traffic jam that caused you to be late. It was not *your fault* there was traffic that caused your delay.

    Your boss, who is usually in by the time you get there, was also delayed and walks in about five minutes after you did. There is no one else in the office, and you are certain that no one even knows you were late. As you sit at your desk, staring at the electronic time sheet, you wonder what harm it would do to simply mark your arrival time as 9:00am. What harm would fifteen minutes do? If you enter your time as 9:00am instead of the actual time of 9:15am, it's justified because it wasn't even your fault, correct? No harm, no foul, right? Wrong! That is what the devil wants you to think. By you misrepresenting your timesheet, you

CHAPTER 6 | THE WEAPONS OF OUR WARFARE

just lied. As innocent as it may appear, it is still a lie.

The Bible says in John 8:44 that the devil is the father of lies. Therefore, when you lie, you give yourself over to him. With this lie, you just granted the devil access to the area of your life the lie speaks of. Meaning, you lied about something dealing with your workplace, which also deals with your finances. Suddenly, you face opposition in the workplace and you lose favor with those who once held you in high regard. You just granted the enemy your workplace as a battleground for him to use against you. You yielded your workplace and your finances over to him, as well, with something as harmless as a little "white lie".

This is how the enemy disarms you and renders your armor ineffective. All he has to do is attack the belt of truth and your whole armor is compromised. Here is another subtle way he does this. Let's take or instance the cashier who mistakenly gives you more money as part of your change. Do you give it back to her, or do you take it and put it away? One time, I was at a deli ordering lunch in NYC. I ordered a sandwich and a 20 oz bottle of Coca-Cola®. She charged me only for the sandwich and not the soda. I did not realize this until I was already walking away with the receipt and my credit card in hand. I reviewed the receipt and turned back around to the cashier to inform her of her oversight. She told me, "It's ok, take it." I thanked her for her generosity, yet, I insisted she charge me for the soda. She was not the owner so she did not have the authority to give me anything in that store for free. There is way more at risk than what we see on the surface.

    Another instance happened recently. My daughter and I were at Walmart. We purchased some items and went through the self-checkout lane to pay for our things. Unknown to either of us, there was an item we overlooked and before we knew it, we inadvertently buried it at the bottom of the cart, covered with the bags of all the items we did purchase. Therefore, we walked out of the store with it. As I loaded the car with the items purchased, I noticed the item, un-bagged at the bottom of the cart. My heart sank.

    I instructed my daughter to finish loading the items in the car's trunk while I returned to the store to pay for this item. I was already in the parking lot. No one knew I had this item. No one would miss it, yet I did what others would not

CHAPTER 6 | THE WEAPONS OF OUR WARFARE

so that I can keep what most don't: my integrity still intact, my armor still in place. I walked back into the store, spoke to the staff, apologized for my oversight, and immediately asked them to ring me up for the item. There is nothing in this world worth the risk of giving something over to the enemy, even if it wasn't intentional. The devil doesn't care that it was a mistake. He sees an open door and will take it. That is what it means to give the devil a foothold. You slightly open the door to an area of your life and he puts his foot there to prevent the door from closing. Soon enough, he makes his way in.

Paul tells us at the beginning of the passage who the enemy is, because he wants us to identify him first. He wants us to see him coming before he can strike. We must resist the devil and he will flee. We serve a faithful God, and he is a God of provision to supply all of our needs. He provides and we don't have to lie to receive it. When we do that, we are inadvertently telling God that we do not trust Him to come through. It is the decisions we make daily that hold our entire armor together. The enemy has always attacked my integrity and the belt of truth because once the belt is off, my whole armor falls apart.

STEAL, KILL & DESTROY

What I learned by reading Chip's book is that there is a practical approach to the armor of God. We just went over the belt of truth. Next in the armor of God is the breastplate of righteousness. The breastplate of righteousness is designed to shield your vital organs against the weapons of the enemy—specifically, your heart. The enemy loves to attack us right where it hurts using matters of the heart. To be righteous means to be in right standing with God. Deuteronomy 6:25 says we do this by observing all of God's commandments. It is impossible for a mere man to do this. We witnessed all throughout the Old Testament as man tried and repeatedly failed. Jesus came to fulfill the Law that we could not. When we accept the gift of salvation, the righteousness of Jesus is transferred unto us. The Bible tells us we are the righteousness of God (Second Corinthians 5:21). I believe that the more we walk in the will of God, the more we are transformed into His likeness. It is when we walk outside of the will of God and pursue the desires of our heart against the will of God that we succumb to the enemy's attack.

CHAPTER 6 | THE WEAPONS OF OUR WARFARE

I remember that I strongly desired to go into full-time ministry because I deceived myself into thinking it was the only way to be effective in His Kingdom. I joined myself to a ministry that was not in God's will for my life and, as a result, suffered an almost fatal wound to my heart. It almost took me out of ministry altogether. I decided not to serve in any official capacity anymore and that I would simply sit in a church pew. I experienced so much condemnation and hurt. The Lord brought my family and I to our current church home and *that* was our healing place; Trinity Church Deltona.

Every Sunday, the Lord ministered to our hearts and after almost a year of sitting, the Lord opened up our hearts to serve again. His ways are always higher, bigger, and better! I was hurt because I had my heart set on serving the Lord how I thought I was supposed to serve Him and lost sight of God's will. Thinking back on it now, there were red flags and indicators that warned me I was out of the will of God, but I ignored the warnings and pursued my own desires.

I am naturally sensitive to the spirit realm and signs that I interpreted as confirmation of being right on track were solely spiritual fabrications of the enemy to keep me sidetracked. It was a shiny substitute for what God had planned all along. It is important to keep your armor up and your spiritual ears open to directions from God. External factors should only serve as a confirmation to what God has already spoken. The sign is not the road, the sign is only a confirmation of the road you are on.

Once you have securely fastened your armor with the belt of truth and your breastplate of righteousness is intact, you are to *"shod your feet with the preparation of the gospel of peace."* This was one of the hardest things for me to comprehend. I did not understand what was meant by the term "the Gospel", so how was I supposed to "shod my feet" with the preparation of it?

The Gospel is the good news, but for whatever reason, I did not really understand what the good news was all about. It wasn't until I made the connection that the good news is that Jesus came and took my place. He died so I can *"have life and have it to the full"* (John 10:10 NIV). I am a sinner and underserving of God's love and grace. I

CHAPTER 6 | THE WEAPONS OF OUR WARFARE

turned my back on God having "known" Him. Yet, I really did not know Him at all. I was serving the Lord because my grandmother did, and so I followed suit. However, whenever I got the choice to decide for myself, I departed from the faith. I said, "No thanks!" to God. The penalty for sin is death. Jesus, who had no sin, took my sin upon Himself simply to save me from the penalty of death. He took my place and was the One who died a violent and gruesome death, instead. When I felt the conviction of my sin and faced the truth of what Jesus did for me, it filled me with relief followed by a surge of joy.

I want to let everyone know what Jesus did for me. I want to share the good news. That is what it means to shod your feet with the preparation of the Gospel. First Peter 3:15 (NKJV) instructs us to "*...always be ready to give a defense to everyone who asks you a reason for the hope that is in you...*". Unashamedly, I proclaim for all who care to hear the reason for my faith and the truth about the redemptive power in the blood of Jesus Christ.

To shod your feet with the preparation of the Gospel of peace means to understand the reason for your faith and be ready to share it at all times.

STEAL, KILL & DESTROY

It is what keeps your feet firmly planted in God. The realization of what the gift of salvation really means to me is what sprung up a desire to serve the Lord wholeheartedly. He is truly my Savior.

> *"Above all, take up the shield of faith with which you will be able to quench the fiery darts of the wicked one"* Ephesians 6:16 (NKJV)

To take up the shield of faith means to trust in God wholeheartedly. Faith comes by hearing and hearing by the Word of God. This faith is not developed overnight. It is through exposure to the Word of God and reliance on the Lord that the shield of faith is strengthened. The bigger your faith, the stronger the shield. Recently, we experienced the threat of a hurricane in Florida.

My family and I live in a small, rented house. The backyard is not completely fenced-in, primarily because there is a swamp in the back that floods with water every time it rains a lot in our area. Recently, it rained heavily every afternoon and the water level rose to where more than half of the backyard was covered in water. One of my coworkers knew of this and a few days

CHAPTER 6 | THE WEAPONS OF OUR WARFARE

prior to Hurricane Dorian's arrival to the Florida coast, she told me she was praying for me.

I thanked her for the prayers as I always welcome prayer. Then, she asked what my plans were to safeguard my home during the hurricane. I replied that my plan was to pray. She said, "Well, I know that, but what is your plan B?" I replied with as much assurance as I have in knowing my own name, "I do not have a plan B, my plan is just to pray and trust in God; that is all I have." Seeing that I was unmoved from my position, she said "ok"; we briefly continued our regular discourse and went about our separate ways.

I shared the story with my husband, and he thought it was funny, because he and my friends all think I have some sort of divine appointment with God that clouds my judgment. He also tried to get me to worry over the hurricane. I refused to listen. I prayed about this hurricane and as I prayed about it, I was reminded about the story of Paul in the book of Acts. When Paul was on a ship in the middle of a storm, an angel of the Lord visited him.

Before the crew set sail, Paul warned the crew of impending danger, but the centurion would not heed his warning. The ship was caught in a storm with hurricane-force winds, which caused them to throw most of their cargo overboard as a preventative measure. In the middle of this storm, Paul was visited by an angel of the Lord who assured him that, while there would be material losses, they would lose no lives. Material things can be replaced, but the assurance that God gives is priceless. What I like most about this passage is how Paul recounts this visit. In Acts 27:23 (NIV) Paul says, *"Last night an angel of the God to whom I belong and whom I serve stood beside me."* Paul emphatically expresses that he belongs to God and, therefore, his fate is in God's hands. That is a good example of what it means to fully trust in God amidst any storm whether physical or spiritual.

I trust what the Word of God says about me. I believe what it says that I am, therefore, whenever the tempest stirs and all might be lost, I am reminded of the God to whom I belong and serve. As a child, people spoke prophetically over my life. Some of those things have not yet come to pass. I believe God will see me through anything that may try to prevent His will for me. God is not a man that he should lie nor the son of man that

CHAPTER 6 | THE WEAPONS OF OUR WARFARE

he should repent, i.e. change His mind about me (Numbers 23:19). God does not take back His gifts (Romans 11:29-31). I believe I will live to see the goodness of God here among the living (Psalm 27:13).

> *And take the helmet of salvation, and the sword of the Spirit, which is the word of God; (Ephesians 6:17 NKJV)*

We put on the helmet of salvation by filling our minds with things of God. Philippians 4:8 (NKJV) instructs us to think on *"whatever things are true, whatever things are noble, whatever things are just, whatever things are pure, whatever things are lovely, whatever things are of good report, if there is any virtue and if there is anything praiseworthy, meditate on these things."*

I think of putting on the helmet of salvation like this. Before I gave my life to the Lord, I frequented night clubs. Before I could enter the club, the bouncer would check my ID. If I did not meet the club's requirement to enter the club, I was not granted entry. Likewise, we must be the bouncer at the "Club of Me." Whenever a thought enters my mind, I immediately ask for its ID. I examine the thought. If it does not meet the criteria of Philippians 4:8, I immediately dismiss the thought; access denied. Simple as that.

The Sword of the Spirit is the Word of God. There is no mistake here when Paul mentions them both in the same verse. The Word of God is what you should fill your mind and heart with. The sword of the Spirit is intended for close quarters combat. When the enemy gets inside your head, it is the Word of God that will push him out. John 14:26 says that the Holy Spirit will help you remember the Word of God. Equip yourself with the Word of God, which is the sword of the Spirit. If you neglect to read the Word for yourself, you will find that you will lose more battles against the enemy in your personal life.

The last thing Paul instructs us to do is to pray *"always with all prayer and supplication in the Spirit, being watchful to this end with all perseverance and supplication for all the saints."* (Ephesians 6:18 NKJV)

First Corinthians 2:11 says no man can know the things of a man except the Spirit of man, which is in him. Likewise, man can never understand the things of God except the Spirit of God. Jesus lives in me as does His Holy Spirit.

CHAPTER 6 | THE WEAPONS OF OUR WARFARE

Sometimes, I set myself to pray, but I am at a loss for words. I do not know how to pray or what to pray for. In moments like these, I pray in the Spirit. The Holy Spirit knows what is at the root of all my problems and knows what the solution to those problems is.

When I do not know how to pray, I pray in the Spirit. Sometimes, I get an understanding of what I am praying for, other times, I do not. But, one thing is certain: I am always invigorated after praying in the Spirit. I find peace and assurance that God heard me, and He's got my back. I do not have to have all the answers; I just need to know where to find them.

CHAPTER 7 | IT IS FINISHED

So when Jesus had received the sour wine, He said, "It is finished!" And bowing His head, He gave up His spirit.
John 19:30

n every story, there is a protagonist and an antagonist. The protagonist is the main character of the story, and the antagonist is the opposing character, or, the villain of the story, if you will. In our story, Jesus is the hero. Usually, whenever you read a story, there is a level of progression before the battle scene and before they crown the hero as victor. What is different in our story is that Jesus already fought the battle and rescued us from certain death. I believe part of the reason we have a peace that surpasses all understanding is because we are resting in the knowledge that the

CHAPTER 7 | IT IS FINISHED

battle is already won. Those who suffer and are bound by the afflictions and cares of this world have yet to arrive to the knowledge and understanding of the fullness of the work that was done on the cross.

If you find that you are struggling in this area and are unsure as to why this is, ask the Holy Spirit to be your guide as I cannot provide you with a definitive answer. I can, however, share with you the reason why I struggled in this area. I am very analytical by nature and sometimes, I need to process all the information firsthand before I can decide. God is wonderful to meet you exactly where you are. I did not see the work firsthand; I just heard about it. I did not see Jesus get beat in person. I wasn't there to watch the anguish on His face when the crown of thorns pierced His brow. I did not see when His clothes were torn from His body exposing His bare skin; I did not see how His head hung low as He wore my shame...*my shame!* I was not there when He looked into the eyes of His mother who suffered in agony at what she witnessed. I was not there! Yet even as I type these words, my eyes water and my heart aches at the realization of how unworthy I am to receive this gift of salvation.

STEAL, KILL & DESTROY

I was not there to witness the progression of the story of Jesus from birth to the Cross. What I have before me is *my life, my pain, my suffering*. Why did I endure the things I did during what should have been the most tender moments of my life? Why did *I* suffer hunger and pain? Why did *I* suffer loss?

Everything you have suffered in your life and everything I have suffered in my life is a direct result of man's will. We sinned and gave access to our adversary into the most vulnerable areas of our lives. He came in swiftly and has ruined many lives, separated holy unions, and flooded our lives with pain and agony. Anguish and torment are his specialty, because it is what awaits him. Some of you are paying for the sins and rebellion of your ancestors because you don't know what you don't know. Deliverance is at hand, but first, you must know you need deliverance.

Many live their lives thinking they do not need deliverance, a hero, or a God. They have made themselves the hero of their story. They may think, *I live a good life. I give to charity. I do not wrong anyone.* Yet, despite all of your good works,

CHAPTER 7 | IT IS FINISHED

know that we have all sinned and have all fallen short of the glory of God. Those things mean nothing if you have not repented and accepted the gift of salvation. Your good works will not prevent you from seeing hell.

Isaiah 64:6 says *"we are all like an unclean thing, and all our righteousness's are like filthy rags; We all fade as a leaf, and our iniquities, like the wind, have taken us away."* Those "works" you think make you better than everyone else or that will save you from a trip to hell are the very ones that will get you there first class. In this verse "filthy rags" refers to the rags women used to use during their menstruation. That is how God sees your good and "self-righteous" deeds. The Pharisees did not see Jesus as the Messiah because their own righteous thoughts blinded them.

Many recovery programs teach that to recover from an affliction or addiction, one must first admit such an affliction exists. To find a solution to the problem, you must first recognize there is a problem. Our problem is the issue of sin. Our sinful nature views sin in the same way most of us view chocolate. There is nothing wrong with a bite here and there. Yet we fail to realize that one bite has long-lasting consequences, not only in your present day, but in the lives of your future generations.

Exodus 20:5-6 (NKJV) says this:

> *5 "... For I, the LORD your God, am a jealous God, visiting the iniquity of the fathers upon the children to the third and fourth generations of those who hate Me,*
>
> *6 but showing mercy to thousands, to those who love Me and keep My commandments."*

Here, God is speaking about idolatry, and in speaking of it, He declares that the children will pay for the sins of the fathers to the third and fourth generation. How long is a generation? A quick Google™ search will yield various answers to that. I believe that a generation on average lasts about 30 years. Multiply that by four and you have 120 years within four generations. What if within those 120 years, another father in your lineage sins and the curse extends down your lineage for another 120 years?

CHAPTER 7 | IT IS FINISHED

The Bible says we have all sinned. David says in Psalm 51:5 (NKJV) *"Behold, I was brought forth in iniquity, And in sin my mother conceived me."*

While it is God's will to redeem us from sin, it is a constant decision to continue a life of sin, despite all of God's plans for our lives. We willingly decide and that is why the evil one comes in and does away with our lives and that of our families. If we want to know the sins of our ancestors, we must inspect our afflictions. Is there a history of alcoholism in our family? Drug addiction? Diabetes? Heart disease? Failed marriages? Most people do not see the importance of knowing their family's history. If we do not learn from the mistakes of our ancestors, we are bound to repeat them. It is important that we study our family trees and expose the underlying roots in order to break the generational chains in the name of Jesus. This way we expose the strongman and take back everything the devil has stolen.

Why do you think doctors are always very interested in not only your medical history but your family history as well? They want to see if you have a predisposition for a specific illness that typically presents itself in your family. If we do this in the natural, why can't we inspect our family trees for the sins we have a predisposition for? It's important to know what afflicted your ancestors so you can know what weapons the enemy has forged against you. The devil does not have any new tricks, he just has experience over you. But you have Jesus and your victory is assured, so put down the Netflix™ and pick up your Bible, which is the sword of the Spirit. Equip yourself with the knowledge to confront that which has afflicted your family for generations. Repent for the sins of your ancestors and claim the blood of Jesus over your life to break these generational curses. You are a chosen generation and a royal priesthood, chosen to set your family tree back on track.

    I am a person of reason and I am explaining to you how God dealt with my reasoning. He enlightened me to the sins of my ancestors who were idol worshipers and delved in witchcraft. He showed me the cause for my suffering as a child. He then showed me my own sins, those no one but He and I knew about. Exodus 34:6-7 (NKJV) says:

CHAPTER 7 | IT IS FINISHED

6 "And the LORD passed before him and proclaimed, "The LORD, the LORD God, merciful and gracious, long-suffering, and abounding in goodness and truth,

7 keeping mercy for thousands, forgiving iniquity and transgression and sin, by no means clearing the guilty, visiting the iniquity of the fathers upon the children and the children's children to the third and the fourth generation."

The emphasis here is on the word "guilty". With my own transgressions, I willingly gave up my future generations to the devil. I was guilty and the never-ending cycle of pain and suffering would continue. God, still dealing with my reasoning, speaks in Ezekiel 18:20 (NKJV):

"The soul who sins shall die. The son shall not bear the guilt of the father, nor the father bear the guilt of the son. The righteousness of the righteous shall be upon himself, and the wickedness of the wicked shall be upon himself."

Likewise, Jeremiah 31:29-34 (NKJV) says this:

29 In those days they shall say no more: 'The fathers have eaten sour grapes, And the children's teeth are set on edge.

30 But everyone shall die for his own iniquity; every man who eats the sour grapes, his teeth shall be set on edge."

31 Behold, the days are coming, says the LORD, when I will make a new covenant with the house of Israel and with the house of Judah—

32 not according to the covenant that I made with their fathers in the day that I took them by the hand to lead them out of the land of Egypt, My covenant which they broke, though I was a husband to them, says the LORD.

33 But this is the covenant that I will make with the house of Israel after those days, says the LORD: I will put My law in their minds, and write it

CHAPTER 7 | IT IS FINISHED

on their hearts; and I will be their God, and they shall be My people.

34 No more shall every man teach his neighbor, and every man his brother, saying, 'Know the LORD,' for they all shall know Me, from the least of them to the greatest of them, says the LORD. For I will forgive their iniquity, and their sin I will remember no more."

What these verses are saying is the good news! While I was bound to my sin, I was a subject in the kingdom of darkness, bound by an evil ruler who delighted in my misery. But there is a new covenant—the game changer! If we confess our sins, God is faithful and just to forgive our sins and cleanse us from all unrighteousness (First John 1:9). God says in Second Corinthians 5:17 that *"...if anyone is in Christ, he is a new creation; old things have passed away; behold, all things have become new"!* With your new identity comes a new address. No longer do you abide in the kingdom of darkness, but you are now transferred into the Kingdom of Heaven and subject to the rule of the Righteous One: The King of Kings and Lord of Lords, Jesus Christ!

For He made Him who knew no sin to be sin for us, that we might become the righteousness of God in Him (Second Corinthians 5:21 NKJV).

Like David, I know I am a sinner and confess my sins one by one as I cry out to the Lord,

> *"Purge me with hyssop, and I shall be clean; Wash me, and I shall be whiter than snow."* Psalm 51:7 NKJV

I am a new creation!

> *We know that whoever is born of God does not sin; but he who has been born of God keeps himself, and the wicked one does not touch him.* First John 5:18 (NKJV)

Once you repent and commit to this walk, it is important to know there is nothing you face that God has not already made a way for. Jesus is fully God and possesses all the attributes of God. He is omnipresent, omnipotent, and omniscient. The miracle in the revelation of Jesus Christ does not require me to know or be a witness to the suffering, or bear witness to His process on the

CHAPTER 7 | IT IS FINISHED

way to the Cross. I now see that while He was enduring His suffering, He fast-forwarded to my suffering.

He saw me when I was alone in a dark room, crying as I sought ways to hide my bruises from the world. He saw the day I hungered and counted pennies so I could feed my child. He saw each blow; He saw how I drowned my sorrows in alcohol and searched for love in empty spaces. He saw me, all of me, as He took up that Cross. Despite the mess, He loved me enough to endure that horrible death just for me. He saw my nothingness and thought I was to die for. He thought I was worth it. He stopped at nothing just to rescue me. And when I wanted to die, He said "I already did so you can live abundantly." That is my God. That is the God I serve. He saw me and He sees you, right there, just as you are. His love is too good to leave you in that state. His love purifies and makes you whole again.

What I have learned in this walk with Christ is that God has already seen all of my tomorrows so there is no need for me to worry or fear. There is no need for me to fight unnecessary battles. Jesus has fought them all. I am victorious in Christ, and I can face whatever this life has to throw at me from the position of a winner. My son has been playing baseball since he was five years old. One thing I would shout from the stands as he goes up to bat is, "You are a winner!" I remind him of his position, despite what curve balls may come. Now, I say the same to you as you face your adversary: *you are a winner*. You might strike out and maybe even hit a foul ball, but you are still at bat, so remember, *you are a winner* until it is time to *go home*.

The End

If you would like to dedicate your life to the Lord or rededicate your life, I have good news! Roman 10:9 says that *"If you declare with your mouth, "Jesus is Lord," and believe in your heart that God raised him from the dead, you will be saved"*! So, repeat after me:

"Jesus, I am a sinner, please forgive me for my sins. I believe that you are the son of God sent to die a horrible death on the cross as a payment for my sins. I believe that you rose again on the third day and that you are seated with the Father in heavenly places. Holy Spirit lead me and guide me in the way that I should go. Thank you, Lord, for saving me, it is a new day, I am a new creation as you live in me. In Jesus name I pray, AMEN!"

Welcome to the winning team ☺!

BIBLIOGRAPHY

"4K." Google Search. Google. Accessed October 26, 2019.
https://www.google.com/search?client=safari&rls=en&q=what+is+4k?&ie=UTF-8&oe=UTF-8.

"Cunning." Google Search. Google. Accessed October 23, 2019.
https://www.google.com/search?client=safari&ei=WbevXY6tN6K6ggea9rHgDg&q=cunning&oq=cunning&gs_l=psy-ab.3..0l10.212899.215648..216041...0.2..0.117.1252.16j1......0....1..gws-wiz.....0..0i71j0i67j0i131.Ee1ziA7GF2A&ved=0ahUKEwjOvd67p7HlAhUineAKHRp7DOwQ4dUDCAo&uact=5.

"FAQs: Plan B One-Step®." FAQs | Plan B One-Step®. Accessed October 23, 2019.
https://www.planbonestep.com/faqs/.

Finochio, Nathan. *Hearing God: Eliminate Myths, Encounter Meaning.* Colorado Springs, CO: WaterBrook, 2019.

Hagin, Kenneth E. *Don't Blame God.* Ken Hagin Ministries, Inc, 2010.

Holy Bible: New King James Version Study Bible, Eggplant/Tan. Place of publication not identified: Holman Bible Pub, 2013.

Ingram, Chip. "Audiobook: Overcoming Emotions that Destroy" July 23, 2015.

Ingram, Chip. *Invisible War: What Every Believer Needs to Know about Satan, Demons, and Spiritual Warfare.* Grand Rapids, MI: Baker Book House, 2008.

"Resentment." Google Search. Google. Accessed October 23, 2019.
https://www.google.com/search?client=safari&ei=3LavXYyhDaOZ_Qa3p7to&q=resentment&oq=resentment&gs_l=psy-ab.3..0l10.123226.124625..124804...0.1..1.202.1067.5j4j1......0....1..gws-wiz......0i71j0i67.7pb-I4dWKvY&ved=0ahUKEwiM_-b_prHlAhWjTN8KHbfTDg0Q4dUDCAo&uact=5.

Sun Tzu. *The Art of War (Amazon Classics Edition)* (p. 6). Amazon Classics. Kindle Edition.

"Temptation." Google Search Google. Accessed October 20, 2019.
https://www.google.com/search?client=safari&ei=wberXZu2E46Hggfph7S4Bw&q=temptation&oq=temptation&gs_l=psy-ab.3..0i67j0i131j0i67l2j0i13l12j0i67l2j0j0i131.43439.48620..48830...0.2..2.257.2020.14j5j1......0....1..gws-wiz.....0..0i71j0i131i67.Zz8fbFBoleg&ved=*The Holy Bible New International Version, Containing the Old and New Testaments.* Grand Rapids, MI: Zondervan Publishing House, 1985.

Tozer, A. W., and David E. Fessenden. The Attributes of God. Camp Hill, PA: Wing Spread Publishers, 2007.

ACKNOWLEDGEMENTS:

I want to thank God for loving me! I thank Him for trusting me with this book and for opening the door for me. I pray that this message reaches the world and that it edifies the body of Christ. Second, I want to thank my husband Reinaldo who is second only to God. I thank him for his support and his love. I thank my children for being my biggest supporters and for listening to me read various versions of this book to them and they caught mistakes that most missed. I want to thank my mom, my sisters, my family and friends who love me unconditionally and support me in their own unique ways. I owe a great amount of gratitude to Evangelist Timothy McCain and his wife Madai who are pastors at Trinity Church Deltona and oversee the Young Adults ministry. Thank you so much for your love, your transparency, your leadership and your support. Most of all thank you for being present. I also want to thank Mark Correll for answering the call to teach and to lead with truth. His bible studies are comprehensive and suitable for today's learner. Be sure to check out his weekly "In the News" broadcasts that are a must watch on YouTube.

In conclusion, I would be remiss not to mention and thank Peter Lopez Jr. who connected me to a wealth of resources that were both instrumental and vital to the production of this book. I want to thank Angel Velez of JRaah Media Group, LLC, who provided such a beautiful cover design; He also created my podcast "So, Tell Me What You Think!"

Last but not least, I thank **YOU** the reader for giving me your time and attention through this journey. Also, if this book has blessed your life, please spread the word by posting a review of this book on Amazon.

Thank you so much, and God Bless ☺

ABOUT THE AUTHOR

Loribel Maldonado was born in Rio Piedras Puerto Rico in 1979. She is the youngest of five girls that were raised by a single mother. During the mid-80's Loribel's family moved to New York City from Puerto Rico. Loribel holds a master's degree in English Literature and she teaches English at a private Christian school. She is a third-year student of Theology at Faith Christian University and expects to graduate in 2020.

You may contact Loribel directly by sending her an email at simplyloribel@icloud.com

RECOMMENDED READINGS:

1. The Holy Bible
2. The Invisible War by Chip Ingram
3. Revelation Bible Study by Mark Correll available only via his website www.markcorell.com
4. Ephesians: Our Blueprint for Maturity by Bob Yandian
5. Growing up Spiritually by Kenneth E. Hagin
6. Knowledge of the Holy by A.W. Tozer
7. The Attributes of God Volumes 1 & 2 by A.W. Tozer
8. Sit, Walk, Stand by Watchman Nee
9. The Believers Authority by Kenneth E. Hagin
10. Bible Prayer Study Course by Kenneth E. Hagin
11. Ever Increasing Faith by Smith Wigglesworth
12. Obedience in Finances by Kenneth E. Hagin
13. The Character of God's Workman by Watchman Nee
14. Changed into His Likeness by Watchman Nee
15. Blessing or Curse: You Can Choose by Derek Prince
16. Hearing God: Eliminate Myths. Encounter Meaning by Nathan Finochio
17. Overcoming Emotions that Destroy by Chip Ingram
18. Destroying the Spirit of Rejection by John Eckhardt
19. Pulling Down Strongholds by Derek Prince
20. Unmasking the Devil by John Ramirez

Lightning Source UK Ltd.
Milton Keynes UK
UKHW020635290123
416118UK00011B/1165